WE DIE STANDING

by

DOM HUBERT VAN ZELLER

True is the instinct in man which salutes
The tiny percentage who die in their boots.

NEW YORK
SHEED & WARD
1949

To

PETER KEARON

<small>AS A SORT OF CRANMORE TOWER</small>

INTRODUCTION

IN WRITING on this and that in the spiritual life I have tried, like the variety programme, to cater for every taste. There are thickish numbers for the serious minded, and some slighter interludes for what is called, obscurely, the general reader. Two of the essays have, in a somewhat different form, appeared in the pages of *The Lock Bulletin*—the editor of which I must thank for letting me include them here—and two more have been preached. Otherwise I think they are all new. On re-reading the MS. I confess to being surprised at the tone of attack which runs through a lot of it. I would like to say in this connexion that any blows which are met with in these pages are primarily aimed at myself. All the more combative passages were occasioned by my saying to myself: "This won't do—it's a misconception (or a mood or a willy) and must be exploded at once." Then I have sat down and written my piece.

CONTENTS

	PAGE
INTRODUCTION	vii
THE EVADED VIRTUE: PENITENCE . . .	I
THE POINT ABOUT PRAYER	8
THE TOUCH OF THE ALCHEMIST	12
SANCTITY	16
ILLNESS	20
IT'S GLAMOUR WE'RE AFTER	25
THE PRAYER-METHOD OBSESSION . . .	29
MORE ABOUT PRAYER	32
THE PECULIAR ENCHANTMENT OF MIDDLE AGE .	36
THE PRAYER OF FUTILITY	39
THE ENGAGEMENT IS ANNOUNCED	44
THE DARK NIGHT OF HOPE	48
THE DARK NIGHT OF CHARITY	52
LONELINESS	56
THE EMOTIONS	61
COMPASSION	66
BUILDING DUNGEONS IN THE AIR . . .	70
THE MISSING LINK	74
HEALTH	81
THE BENEFIT OF THE DOUBT	85
TRUE AND FALSE REST	92

		PAGE
MORE ABOUT REST	. . . . . .	96
POSSESSIVENESS	. . . . . .	99
CONTEMPLATION	. . . . .	103
THE PRAYER OF PETITION	. . . . .	106
ON BEING BOGUS	. . . . .	109
SHEPHERD AND SHEEP	. . . . .	112
BLACK SHEPHERDS OF THE FAMILY	. . .	116
MISPLACED PERSONS	. . . . .	119
WORK	. . . .	122
SERVICE-FLAT CIVILIZATION	. . . .	125
FRIENDSHIP: THE GENERAL IDEA	. . . .	128
FRIENDSHIP: SOME FURTHER ASPECTS	. . .	133
FRIENDSHIP: THE TRANSITION PERIOD	. . .	136
GENEROSITY	. . . . . .	141
DEATH: OTHER PEOPLE'S	. . . . .	145
DEATH: OUR OWN	. . . . .	149
PRAYER: A QUESTION OF ANGLE	. . . .	152
YOUTH	. . . .	155
WHY NOT TRY THE GOSPEL?	. . . .	159
ERECTI MORIAMUR	. . . . .	163

THE EVADED VIRTUE: PENITENCE

THE OLD TESTAMENT is always telling us to do penance: the Prophets spoke about little else. The New Testament repeats the same call: St. John the Baptist and our Lord are as emphatic as their predecessors. Penance was practised by the saints, is written about by the authorities, is (on occasions—notably during Lent) preached from the pulpits. Then we look around and ask ourselves: yes, but is it—by the ordinary run of Catholics—ever done?

There is a whole catalogue of evils which can be cast out only by prayer and fasting; the "and fasting" is apt to be overlooked. "Will it do if I give up sugar in coffee after lunch?" Will it do what? It won't move mountains or bring about the conversion of England, but perhaps it will do something. At all events it will show that there is a realization of the necessity of penance, and it is precisely this that is so conspicuously lacking in the milk-and-barley-water Christianity of to-day. Still more is it lacking, of course, in the neo-paganism which exists in Christian countries but outside the Christian churches. After all, the ancient pagans had their sacrifices; the moderns recognize no need for the placating of their gods.

There is no escaping it: where there is sin there has to be sorrow for sin. Effective sorrow, not mere sentiment. When a nation has sinned, it has to humble itself afterwards and ask pardon. How many nations even admit sin—let alone beg to be forgiven? This book is not going to be an indictment against nations; it sets out to enquire into, and assist, the mind of the individual. But the individual conscience can't always be separated from the corporate

conscience, and sometimes we see our personal responsibility more clearly when shown up in the light of the
responsibility of the whole. Appeal after appeal has come to
us in our own time to do public penance, and it is worth
considering whether as individuals we are entirely free from
blame for the conditions around us.

It is not always the voice of a prophet that is used by God
to call a wayward people to its senses. A crisis of some sort
can be made to serve instead. Intelligent beings should be
able to find out, from the events which shake and shape their
world, which way the wind is blowing. This generation
has seen crisis following crisis—the word itself means
"judgement"—and men have deliberately not asked themselves where the wind was coming from and why it was
being blown. We have been warned by the findings of
the scientists and the forecasts of the economists. We have
been warned by the farmers, the doctors, the politicians.
Even the weather has been a warning to us. A Judgement.
And we say we have not been warned by God.

"Oh, but all these things would have happened in any
case. It's absurd to put them down to an Almighty with
an avenging sword in one hand and an hour-glass with the
sands running out in the other. Besides if He'd wanted to
pull us up, why didn't He speak to us through the mouth of
one of His servants as He did in the Bible, or by means of
miracles?" In the first place, would these things have happened in any case? God uses natural means to bring about
His supernatural plan, and it looks very much as if the world
has been asking for punishment. Absurd to think of God
threatening mankind? Why absurd? He's done it before
—and with much the same sort of sword. Threats of war,
famine, dispossession, social and economic collapse . . .
there is nothing very new about this. While if we want to
hear Him speaking through the mouths of His servants we

have only to listen and we shall hear the refrain repeated time
and time again. But we don't listen. The Pope has preached
repentance. Our Lady has appeared to a number of people
and told them that the time has come for penance or there
will be trouble for mankind. Lourdes was primarily a
call to penance; the invitation to be healed came second.
Père Lamy clamoured for a change of heart, for repentance.
"Do penance," he said, "or there will be war." And there
was war. The message from Fatima was even more explicit:
the time is getting short . . . do penance or Russia will rule
the West. Our Lady is appearing in Belgium: her preaching
is everywhere the same. We can't say we haven't heard. If
we want the tide to turn we know what we have to do. But
we are still dancing on the shore with our backs to the
waves.

Now to leave the general need for the particular one: the
place of mortification in the life of the individual soul. It
used to be considered axiomatic that the spiritual edifice
rested upon the twin supports of prayer and penance. But
twins have a way of growing up unevenly. For every
twenty sermons or articles on prayer, there probably isn't
more than one on penance. (Look, for instance, at the
chapter headings of any spiritual book—this one included.)
The raising of the heart gets its measure of attention; the
afflicting of the flesh—both as a subject and as a practice—is
left to the ancients. This escape from penance takes two
forms, and both of them have the backing of excellent
reasons. We will deal with each in turn.

In the first place prayer is claimed to be a more *spiritual*
thing than penance. It is higher and nobler, and will be
continued in heaven long after penance has been done away
with. Prayer unites us positively with God, and therefore
must be given far more attention than penance which is at
best a negative affair, a going against self. Prayer looks

upward and outward, expressing love, desire, hope . . .
while penance looks back, expressing contrition for past
failure. Prayer offers to God the soul: penance offers only
the body. Now all this is true enough as far as it goes, but
the point is not which of the two is the *better*, but how to get
the best out of each. It might be argued that to think is more
noble than to eat, but the point is that we need to do both.
In our preference for prayer we are inclined to leave out of
account the fact that though penance may be less important
than prayer, it is also far less pleasant. We should remember,
moreover, that if penance is being practised as it should be,
it *is* an act of prayer—positively uniting us with the Passion,
positively expressing love, positively surrendering self. In
fact, if penance is not found to be actively bringing the soul
nearer to God it had better not be practised at all: it is a sheer
waste of energy: much better be employed in something
else. "Will it *do* if I give up etc." misses the main idea.
The second line of argument which is used for avoiding the
more uncomfortable forms of mortification is based on the
supposition that the human race is declining in stamina, and
that therefore the austerities which were all very well for
our ancestors are happily inappropriate to-day. This
consoling theory finds expression in slightly differing
formulae: asceticism must keep in step with the development
of man's cultural activity and the increasing refinement of
his nature. That's the first one. Next: the rough type pro-
duced in the Middle Ages required a correspondingly rough
system of control, and where the simpler, more objective
mind of former times was able to take self-inflicted punishment in its stride, we, introspective and leaning more and
more upon the conclusions of psychologists, are liable to see
in voluntarily chosen pain something rather morbid. Then
there's this one: the darknesses of prayer which the mystics
of the present day are always talking about must be very

much more purifying than all the chains and flagellations of the older tradition. These catch phrases—and there are others—all add up to the same thing: namely that the appeal of St. John the Baptist no longer applies, and that when our Lord spoke about the necessity of everyone doing penance ("or you shall all likewise perish"—in the way that those perished upon whom the tower of Siloe fell), He didn't really mean it.

Take the objections one by one as they are set out above. It has yet to be proved that the present generation is less physically robust than those that have gone before. One would have thought that the war might have exploded this theory. It looks as if people's powers of endurance are as good now as ever they were; and as for nerves—if it is on the mental side that our weakness is supposed to lie—there have been nerves in every age. By the way people speak it might be supposed that neurotics were something new in the history of mankind. If there is any truth in this idea of a declining stamina, physical and mental, it is that by letting ourselves down gently, we of this generation have come to dislike physical hardship more, and that by exploiting our nervous upsets we have created a wider field for nervous disorders. It is only a pity that we have met with a wider sympathy. A case of demand and supply. The bigger the nursing home, the more people to put in it.

Further: to rule out self-inflicted punishment on the grounds that "the whole thing is probably rather unhealthy when you get down to it . . . probably suppressed sex or something of that sort", is to throw countless generations of saints under a darkening and quite ridiculous suspicion of sadism. If it is the fanatical excesses of Buddhism that we are afraid of, we in this country have little cause to be alarmed: there is something preventatively un-English about Thibet. Nor is it easy to see why the danger of extravagance is so

much more to be feared with regard to corporal penance
than with regard to these interior penances which we hear
so much about. If there is risk attaching to body-culture,
there is certainly much more risk attaching to culture of the
spirit. By all means mortify curiosity, vanity, uncharity
and the rest, but these should be mortified anyway. Morti-
fications of an interior kind may be both more necessary
and more sanctifying, but that—as in the discussion above
regarding the relative merits of prayer and penance—is not
the point. The point is that if the flesh is not mortified *as
well* it will get the upper hand of the spirit. One or the other
has got to be in control.

To the people who say that the state of their prayer
provides them with all the mortification they need, it might
be suggested that though prayer may be very mortifying—
and while it nearly always is—it doesn't *hurt*. Penance does.
Or should do. The worst that we get in prayer is boredom,
and most of us do not shrink from boredom as we shrink
from downright pain. The feeling that our prayer is a
complete waste of time is humiliating in the extreme and is
very good for us, but it is a feeling we cannot escape. It is
allowed us by God to test our fidelity. We can't suddenly
decide not to feel it. Whereas here we are discussing
penance: humiliations and sufferings undertaken in a spirit
of atonement and with a view to sharing *from choice* in the
sufferings of Christ. Aridities in prayer, because they are
sent to us by God, are obviously more advancing to the
spiritual life than anything we can hit upon in the way of
selecting tortures—there can clearly be no comparison between the relative value of God-sent and man-devised
crosses—but the point I am trying to make here is that we
can never afford wholly to discard the crosses that are
voluntary, though we must never take them up without the sanction of advice and the approval of those

responsible for our souls—otherwise they may do more harm, spiritually, than good.

In the end we come back to the axiom with which we started, and say that the balance must be maintained between prayer and penance. Prayer without penance is liable to become a culture; penance without prayer is liable to become an obsession. Prayer is not to be dabbled in as a rare and precious hobby (if there is one dilettante who is wholly objectionable it is the dilettante mystic), while penance is not to be wallowed in as a misery or an advertisement. Prayer and penance safeguard one another, help one another out, express one another. Like Gilbert and Sullivan, each is incomplete on its own.

Though we may not feel called by God to embrace the camel-hair of St. John the Baptist, we should occasionally examine our wardrobe on the question of soft garments. Garments have a way of becoming softer and softer. So have we.

THE POINT ABOUT PRAYER

PEOPLE are apt to make two mistakes about prayer: they either imagine it to be so easy that they can manage it at once, or else so difficult that it is not worth while going on with. The answer is that because it is open to all it can't be very difficult, and because it is part of the burden of religion it can't be very easy. Whether we find it difficult or easy we have got to do it, so the more we get ourselves used to the practice and the less we worry about our reactions to it the better. But taken all in all it is perhaps more satisfactory to think that prayer is going to be easy than to think it is going to be difficult, because it means that we shall at least start off. If we look only at the difficulties we are handicapped by discouragement before we begin. And right the way through this business of prayer there is nothing that acts as a more formidable obstacle than discouragement. So it will be mainly about this that the following paragraphs are concerned.

St. Paul's "Pray without ceasing" should provide the answer to those who are weighed down by the sense of their insufficiency. The saint is not exhorting to the almost impossible. He is telling every one—even the people who feel they are no use at it and that for them it is a complete waste of time—that their whole life can become a prayer. "You must make a habit of prayer," St. Paul is telling us, "and to make a habit of anything you must repeat and extend the act." First easy acts, then difficult ones. It is like learning a language: easy to make oneself understood, difficult to become really fluent. The way to become fluent is to practise often. Prayer is learned by repeated acts.

There is no short cut to a habit. A resolution to go on once one has begun is not a short cut. It is a good start but it is not a short cut. A method learned from a book is not a short cut. It may be a further step towards acquiring the habit, but it is not a short cut. A book of meditations is not a short cut. It is a guide to fall back upon when the habit is wearing thin, but it is not a short cut. In other words there is no substitute for the work of cultivating the habit of prayer. You have to do the thing before you can live the thing. And in order to do the thing properly you not only have to be faithful to your purpose but you have to be ruthless in the treatment of your feelings. You must not allow yourself to judge of the success or failure of your effort by whether you feel the presence or absence of devotion. What we feel, after all, is only the result of the effect of conditions on matter. The whole point about prayer is the effect it has on God. Our feelings will give us no true estimate of this.

Though there may be difficulty connected with forming the habit of prayer, there is no habit so easily drawn upon once it is there. So habitual can prayer become that the natural movement of the mind is towards God instead of towards creatures. I say "natural" movement and not "automatic" movement, because for prayer to have any value it must be non-mechanical. There is all the difference in the world between an instinctive direction of the soul and a purely routine action. St. Antony may have said that a man's prayer is still imperfect while he remembers that he prays, but he would never have said that the perfect man need not remember *to* pray. We don't begin our prayer, however brief and spontaneous, without some sort of desire to do so. Intention is necessary even if attention escapes us. Desire for God is the condition of prayer, and very often recollection is nothing else than that. Awareness of God's presence is not always prayer—the sinner can be aware of God's presence and rebel against it—but the desire for God's glory always is. And to become a man of prayer it is necessary so to extend this desire that it becomes habitual.

"Am I to believe then," it might be asked, "that as long as I have the general intention of praising God, I can have as many distractions as I like?" "As many as you get," would be the answer, "not as many as you like." Once we start liking a distraction enough to follow it up, it is a distraction in the fully guilty sense. But if we haven't been made aware of the fact that it is going on, if we had no intention of pursuing it once we knew it was there, if we have no intention of letting go the thought of God, if in other words we have no affection for the wretched thing even though we can't help being interested in it while it is there, then, though we may spend half an hour in thinking all round it, there is nothing in the least bit wrong in having had it. Fortunately this is a fact which has been stressed by present-day writers, and most people are prepared to believe it. What people are less prepared to believe is that not only is a prayer not wasted when it is distracted but that it may be, on account of the distractions, a better prayer. It is better for the humiliation which its obvious insufficiency occasions. If there is one disposition more necessary than the determination to go on with it, it is the disposition of feeling that you are so bad at it that it hardly seems worth while if you do. If you persevere in the prayer of stupidity, unable to fix your mind on holy things for the entire time of your prayer, and feeling throughout that you are the last person who should be attempting this sort of thing, and that though you seem to be at the mercy of distractions which you can't for the life of you remember afterwards but which you hate having, then you are doing what countless

people have done before you and exactly what God wants
you to be doing at the present moment.

The worry about being distracted can itself become such
a distraction that the whole business is complicated far
more than it need be. This is not to suggest that distractions
should be admitted on the grounds that the effort to get
rid of them is more distracting than the distractions themselves, it is merely to point out that the whole of the soul's
energy in prayer should not be expended in driving away
these maddening cross-currents of thought: love is the
occupation of the soul, not struggle. Banishing distractions
can become the preoccupation. The same situation can
arise outside prayer time as regards bad thoughts: we can
become obsessed with the necessity of suppressing them
and so become involved in the thoughts themselves. In
the case of distractions, as in the case of bad thoughts,
the safest thing is to turn calmly towards God in the depths
of the soul, and to tell Him that whatever is going on near
the surface is no concern of ours . . . we despise and re-
pudiate the disturbance, and we are not going to let ourselves get worked up about it. In this way we by-pass the
unruly elements, delaying at them only for as long a time as
it takes to assure ourselves that they are powerless to delay
us. If we can habituate ourselves to the knowledge that
what goes on without our consent in the sensitive part of
the soul is no obstacle to progress, the spiritual life loses
many of its problems. What we have to do is to make ourselves responsible for the citadel of the soul, asking God to
see to the dispositions for us, and not to work ourselves into
a nervous state about what is going on in the outskirts.
Serious rebellions seldom start in the suburbs. The only
distractions which we have reason to fear are those that we
have admitted to the mind.

THE TOUCH OF THE ALCHEMIST

THERE are some natures who seem, without obviously missing anything, to jog along for years and yet never appear to be fully alive. Often they don't feel the emptiness in the least, and it is not as if they were complete failures, because there is frequently a measure of outward achievement in their lives which preserves them from any sense of inferiority. It is just that you feel they are not very vital. They are like those Dutch canal paintings: good and solid but crying out for the brush of a Monet or a Sisley. Then into the lives of these good ordinary people comes some sudden shock, a clean cut, and the whole thing changes. Nothing is the same at all. They light up, they expand, they begin to live. Other people notice it. Every one can see that Monet has gone over the canvas: the canals are shimmering, the poplars rustle. The people themselves in whom this transformation has taken place look back and wonder how they could have existed for so long on such boring interests, how they could have been content to run on one cylinder. They were hungry before but they didn't know it. They are hungry now but they know that their appetite is a healthy one. Without being in the least bit starved they hunger for life—natural, intellectual, spiritual. Their desire is to give to life and not only to get from it. Life from now on must be scattered with both hands. Energy must be generated. They must turn themselves inside out and meet mankind more than half-way. Existence is not enough, life must be something much more positive. You get an illustration of the process in Maurice Baring's book *Daphne Adeane*.

What is it that can produce this sudden reorientation? Why do some people never seem to experience it? Are we among those who are still trailing along in low gear? Have we missed our chance? Have we blinded ourselves to the light which even now may be shining through the stained-glass window? Have we been too lazy to look up and see colour where before we saw only panes of dingy grey?

Perhaps there *are* souls who are by nature more negative than positive, remaining always rather flat and non-conducting, neither wanting much from life nor giving it, content to leave the world as they found it without making any appreciable impression upon it and expecting it to make even less upon them. There *may* be such souls, but let us hope there are precious few. Few, anyhow, who end up like that.

Once in hospital I had for a nurse one who had been through two wars, who had travelled, had worked in every sort of hospital, mixed with every sort of person. Yet she seemed to see no farther than the out-patients' department. Finding that she had been in Spain right through the Revolution I asked her what opinion she had formed of the Spanish people, and what were her impressions of the country generally. She thought for a long time before answering my question—clearly the idea of forming impressions was new to her—and then said this: "What struck me was the way their medicine glasses were shaded pink."

If people don't look they simply do not see. Quite so. But what is it that makes some people simply not *look*? Is it lack of imagination? Lack of education? Lack of direction? Certainly it is not lack of things to look at. All sorts of absorbingly interesting things are constantly passing along the horizon, and the absurd part of it is that we let them pass. We don't give them a thought. We don't bother to look. And then if we are lucky something or someone comes

along, and, as I say, the landscape bursts into flower. It is
unlikely that a book would be powerful enough to effect the
transformation, but it has been known to happen as the result
of a retreat. A complete change of work and environment
would be more likely to do it, though it would have to be
the kind of change which calls for such re-adjustments as
we would ordinarily never have the generosity or enterprise
to make. Sometimes a long illness will release the spring;
enforced leisure has a way of bringing the soul up against the
supreme issues, forcing it to face reality. Far more frequently
of course than in the cases mentioned it is by coming across
a person that the soul receives a new start. You see it in
history, you see it in the world of art, of music, of letters:
the dumb man is introduced to the right personality and
straightway the string of his tongue is loosed. Fortunate for
the one born dumb if this happens early on in his career.
You see it often in schools. A boy who is written off by the
authorities as a dead loss stumbles upon somebody who
gives him confidence, somebody who holds out an ideal,
somebody who represents a whole lot of perhaps quite
indefinable things which are felt to be worth striving for.
Father Bede Jarrett had a particular genius for evoking this
response. He dug up clay, and handed it over alabaster. The
influence need not necessarily come from one much older, it
can come from someone of the same age. In some ways it is
better that a boy's heroes should be of his own generation;
but whoever it is that opens the new window on his life it
has to be someone who believes in him, and, what is as
important, who makes him believe in himself.

In later life the enchantment is different but the principle
is the same. It is now not so much a following of someone's
lead—taking the colour and advice of a man one admires—
as a process whereby one is shaken out of one's rut by the
force of a new emotion. A man who falls in love with

someone who is both more holy and more alive than he is, is subjected willy-nilly to changes of vision which he would never have dreamed of as being possible. All sorts of things he had not realized before, or realized only in theory, become true. He suddenly finds that he is no longer a unit; he is a person. He no longer drifts along the sidewalk of life as part of the crowd; he has direction, purpose, plan. He no longer sees things as a succession but as a pattern; not as a grey blur but as a flaming riot of colour; not as the result of a necessary and remote collection of laws in the outcome of which his life is as insignificant as it is unquestioned, but as the spontaneous and unique dispensation of providence whereby he is singled out to enjoy the intimate ecstasies of being alive. He sees the inwardness of creatures as well as the beauties of their outwardness, and, if he has learned the lesson that his experience is meant to teach him, he refers them back again gratefully to God. He, in short, wakes up. And blessed are they to whom is given the power of waking people up.

To conclude. We must not only see but look; not only look but point out to others. Such was the vision of the saints: communicative and not for private view only. The saints were like magnifying glasses, bringing to light the subtle loveliness of whatever came along, whether of nature, of grace, or of art. They were God's showmen. Nor is this surprising since more clearly than the rest of mankind the saint sees things through the eyes of God. He discovers for himself and then for others the good that God sees in His creatures, the good that all too often is seen out of focus by the creatures themselves. The saint looks for the best and finds it. He knows it is there. Even when it is hidden his faith gives him vision. He has confidence. "Lord," let us cry with the blind man of Jericho, "that I may see." And, having seen, be ready to share my vision with others.

SANCTITY

IT IS sobering to think that some who have worked miracles, helped countless souls, received supernatural graces in prayer, have gone off the rails and died outside the Church. But it works both ways: there are sinners who have made good and ended up as saints. And fortunately there are far more among this second group than among the first. What is it, we ask ourselves, that can alter the apparently settled course of a man's life like this? Not merely alter it but turn it right about so that the soul races along in the opposite direction? One can understand the man who can't quite bring himself to be really good and who gradually reduces the pressure until the ideal of high sanctity is shelved. One can also understand the man who tires of sin, is even disgusted with himself for having dabbled in it, and who decides to live a decent, if not a heroic, Christian life. What we want to know is the process whereby a near-saint becomes a renegade, and a near-devil becomes bent on sanctity.

First as to what this process does not involve. It is not, in the case of the holy man gone wrong, a withdrawing of grace on God's part. Nor, in the bad man's conversion, is it a compulsion of grace. The grace is there in either case—for the soul to use if he chooses. Nor is it *directly* a question of conduct—in the way of sins on the one hand or in the way of virtuous acts on the other. Acts of sin lead to a life of sin, and so in that sense sin of course accounts for apostasy. In the same way good acts build up a character of goodness which will ultimately lead on to heroic sanctity. But the point I am trying to make is that it is the mind behind the sin and the good act that qualifies. The difference between the sinner and the saint is not primarily one of acts or even habits but one of consent and desire. The big moment is not when a man sins but when a man surrenders to the direction of his sin. If he accepts his sin, lies down under it, associates himself with it, then he is done. He has made room for it in his life, he has excused it, it is an accepted part of him. Until this happens, and so long as he knows that he can and should fight against it and win, so long as he has not admitted it to the citadel of his soul, he is safe. Or at all events he is savable.

The saint is the same in reverse: he sees that God wants to be the supreme influence in his life, and he not only allows this but furthers it all along the line. To every urge that comes from God he assents, and to every suggestion of evil he presents an uncompromising refusal. Such is his settled will. Of course he will fail, but when he does so he feels a complete cad, and renews his intention of loving God beyond all else. It is not his failures that disqualify him—they do not even seriously discourage him—it is only if he were content to fail that his sanctity would be imperilled. But the true saint never is content to fail. He knows that he is liable to fail, he accounts it a mercy of God that he doesn't fail more often, he is humbled but not disconsolate when he has failed. He never accepts his failure with shrug-shouldered indifference, telling himself that after all every-one else does much the same thing and that one can't be expected to be perfect. Which is what we do. Dare we look into our lives and say that there is no imperfection for which we have a liking? A habit of self-indulgence which we felt vaguely uncomfortable about at one time but which we admitted into our life and which we now take for granted? We have got so used to it that we hardly bother to make excuses for it. We can't think of ourselves without it. How does this apply to an affection, for instance, which we know to be ill-regulated but which has become part of us? A form of work? An ambition? A piece of information which we know we should impart but which we have withheld for so long that it has become a guilty secret? There was none of this about the saints. Never for a moment did the saints adjust their standards to the street level of their failures.

The mistake we make is to look at the statistics of a person's life—what he's done. But just as an artist is not an artist only when he is painting, so a saint is not a saint only when he is performing saintly acts. He may be more saintly then than at other times—just as an artist is most an artist when at his proper job—but the thing is a *life*, not a lot of acts strung together.

The beauty of this saint-life is that it can be embarked upon at any moment. We don't have to wait for a miracle: the grace is there. The sin-life is there too. It is a matter of setting the soul. Most of us are, in the language of the barometer, set fair. At times we vary from "cloudy" to "storm", but even "fair" is not good enough: there must be more than bright intervals in our lives, we must live in the light of the sun. Live in it and die in it. Holiness is never giving up the search for God. If right up to the end we are found wanting madly to do God's will—even though we may not be very clear as to what it is, or (more likely still) may not have done it very well—we shall have achieved the main purpose of our lives. To desire God's will is to have discovered it, and to have desired it sufficiently is to have performed it. What more could be asked of any soul?

I once gave a retreat to the junior part of a boys' school. After urging the young men (eight and nine years old) to the heights, I was told by one of them in an interview afterwards that though sanctity might suitably be attempted later on it was clearly uncalled for just yet. Two weeks later I was giving a retreat to some business men in London, and again I made a spirited bid for a response to the call of real holiness. In an interview afterwards I was told by a retired stockbroker that had I put forward this scheme twenty years earlier there might have been something in it but that now of course one was too old to start. It seems hard on God that there should be closed seasons in sanctity. If one lot of people are too young and another lot are too old, when exactly *is* man ready for the effort? The chances are that I shall stiffen with my years, but I shall know in my heart that if the vision is dimmed, it will be of my own dimming. So help me, God.

ILLNESS

"I WILL die on my feet," said Vespasian, "as becomes an Emperor." For the word Emperor we can substitute Christian, or simply man: "as becomes a man." It certainly does become a man to go on to the end, especially if you are the kind of man who bears the name of Christ. But you will find it very difficult to do. Not that your determination, made with a gay Vespasian flourish, will necessarily weaken, but simply that so many things will come along and spoil it all. If you are a business man, your firm will have got rid of you on the first evidence of a decline; if you are a religious, your superior will have relieved you of your work long before you have worn yourself out in it; neither have the Services, any more than the legal or medical professions, any room for a sick man; if you are on your own—say a painter or a writer—your family will have you between the sheets with a hot water bottle before your temperature has reached a hundred; and even if you are a jolly tramp, with every right, one would have thought, to die on the road or in a field, you will find that the State will appear in time to mess it up. Apart from accident or death in battle, it has become uncommonly difficult to die in harness—even if you are a horse.

So it is really a matter of steeling yourself to meet your last illness in a nice tough frame of mind and not snivelling your way into it with every excuse your self-pity can advance for lying down. Not only your last illness, *all* illness. "As becomes an Emperor, I will be sick standing up." It doesn't read so well but the sentiment rings true.

It is the authentic thing. As it is the authentic thing, as it is
in the tradition, when the Christian says "I'm not going to
give God *only* what He asks for". The Christian must be
ready to lay down his life when and where and how God
wants him to do so. Well, let him do it in a big way for God.
Let him do it with an air. The Christian—that is the
follower of Christ—who is looking up nursing homes on
the south coast the moment he feels a chill coming on is a
misconception. He strikes a false note.

Very good then: we have got our patient, protesting
vigorously and with a raging temperature, to bed. What is
his attitude now? His attitude must be one of absolute and
childlike abandonment. Abandonment to the authorities, to
circumstance, to the will of God. One of the great ad-
vantages of being ill, and there are many, is that perhaps for
the first time in our life we are forced to become passengers
in the race of life—literally patients and not assertives. We
are so used to being masters of our affairs that it does us the
world of good to be for a time subjects of inescapable
circumstance. The inescapable circumstance, however, is
only of supernatural value to us when we accept it as the will
of God. There are many who love God, but not so many
who love His will. God's will is to be found most surely in
every illness, however slight. In illness we are at the mercy
of others, dependent on others for everything, with all the
merits of holy obedience and all the opportunities of
religious detachment.

In the ordinary run of health we rely for our spiritual
lives very much upon our own tried systems. To a certain
extent we lean upon the advice of our confessor, but
directors seem to be going out, and more and more it is the
individual who regulates his life to-day. We have, at any
rate, our own devotions, our own ascetical practices, our
rules for this and that. Years perhaps have gone to the

building of an observance from which it would be in-
conceivable that we should part. Confessors may have
sanctioned it, even vows may have sanctified it, time and
habit and possibly a gradual but perceptible progress may
have justified it. It is our prop, it is our ladder, it is *us*.
Then comes a first-class illness and the prop is kicked away,
the ladder is thrown down, we find ourselves turning
somersaults in mid-air. But all this is excellent because it
means that now we *have* to rely on God and God alone.
Not now on any self-devised system of service but on God
Himself. And our doing so *is* service. This reliance, this
acceptance of His inescapable will, is far more sanctifying,
because less showy, than any spectacular heroics of our own
choosing. We cannot recite the prayers we are accustomed
to, we are not allowed to do penance, we are not sure of
being able to receive Holy Communion, holy books are
almost certainly denied us, we find it impossible to collect
our thoughts and focus them on God, and we are always
losing count in the rosary. There is nothing we can offer to
God but ourselves and our illness. There is nothing we can
do but go on as we are. Before, while enjoying health, we
liked seeing what we were making of the spiritual life. Now
we see nothing. Before, we liked to think of ourselves as
buzzing about with good works on our capable hands. Now
we don't like to think of ourselves at all. It is very salutary,
very humbling.

One of the drawbacks, humanly speaking, of being ill
is that our judgement lets us down. We fail to appreciate
in the intellect many things which it would be of infinite
consolation to us to feel in the will. Many truths which
we would have been able to discourse upon at length if we
were well, seem now to be just beyond the rim of our
experience. And even, which is perhaps more disturbing,
beyond the rim of our interest.

So we lie there wishing—stupidly of course—that we could be doing God's will properly instead of having to waste time in this ridiculous way. We forget the positive opportunities which this apparent waste of time affords: the patience with which we can approach the annoyances of our treatment, patience with those in charge of us, with visitors who stay too long, with diet, with sleeplessness, with boredom, with loneliness, with downright pain. "Oh yes, there's *that* I suppose, but I'm doing it so badly that it can't possibly compensate for what I'm missing." It's this, isn't it—the sense of lost opportunity and the feeling of present insufficiency—that weighs upon us? We feel it as being worse than the illness itself. We think of the letters we might be writing to help people, we think—if we are priests—of the retreats we have had to cancel and the converts whom we would be instructing but who have had to be put on to someone else who will not do the work nearly so well; we sicken at the thought of what those are doing who depend upon us to keep them out of trouble; we long to get up and go to the rescue of souls whom we feel to be quite incapable of resisting temptation without our assistance. How foolish all this is, and what a complete delusion. It is sheer pride to regard ourselves as being of so much use in the world, and sheer want of trust to imagine that God won't take care of our work in our absence. God loves souls infinitely more than we do, and it is not likely that He will allow them to be handicapped spiritually by anything so unavoidable (from our point of view) and foreseen (from His) as an illness. Besides we can do from our beds far more for souls than we could ever be doing from our actual contacts. Anxieties such as we have described can become an obsession. We must tell ourselves that the moral life of the universe is not conditioned by our influence. We have the desire to serve God and souls: the form this takes must be left to God. If we are trying to practise the perfection proper to the invalid we have no reason to worry. The trouble is that we worry so much about the perfection which we are not able to practise that we forget about the perfection which we are. "The effort to do great things," says Seneca, "is a great thing in itself." Where great things are out of the question we have to content ourselves with the effort. And where making the effort is out of the question—as it is in most illnesses—we have to content ourselves with the desire to be making it if we could. This is not so glamorous, but it is, so the authorities tell us, as effective. Not even the worst kinds of illness debar us from the longing for God, and though we may feel we are doing this badly, there is always the consolation that if we felt we were running our illness well it would be doing us more harm than good. And God sends us our illnesses to do us good.

Recently I visited a man in hospital who had been in bed for seven months and had had a series of operations. "I've learned a lot," he said. "I wouldn't have missed it for anything." But then he wasn't suffering from the worst kind of illness. The worst kind of illness is the one where there is nothing the matter with us. It needs almost a miracle to get anything good out of that kind. And another miracle to cure it.

IT'S GLAMOUR WE'RE AFTER

WELL, isn't it? The other day Arnold Lunn, with that generous smile of his which means battle, said to me: "The difference between you wretched modern artists and the ancients is that they used their talents to boost beauty while you use beauty to boost your beastly talents." If this is true, it means that painters are not only out to give glamour but are also out to get it. Nor is the twofold tendency confined to the painting world. You and I, we are all in it. The writing world knows it won't find a public unless its books are humming with sex; the acting world can't afford to rely upon ability without looks; music, education, human intercourse, sermons even, and certainly politics have to be hotted up to suit the jaded palate of a generation which likes its piecrust but which has precious little use for the pie. Anything more solid than froth is judged too heavy for human endurance. Worthiness is at a discount. Earnestness is ridiculed. The sterling has little market value; it is paper virtue that is recognized in modern currency. What people admire and envy in others is the power to dazzle. If the dazzling qualities happen to be virtues at the same time so much the better. But the main thing is the dazzle, not the virtue. "When you are introduced to someone, what do you look for first?" "That he should be amusing." Perhaps it is only the saints that look for understanding, for response to the divine spark, for humility, for a flaming idealism, for sincerity, for self mistrust, and so on in those they meet. But it is a rather revealing commentary upon oneself if the first

25

thing one hopes to find in somebody new is something funny.

But perhaps this test is too searching. In which case leave the new acquaintance, who in any case is expected to show himself in good form and has to be sized up accordingly, and take the question of what it is that people admire in their friends. For years I have been asking young men this question—it irritates them madly—and the answers which I have received have been illuminating. For one thing I find that the answers I get now are different from the answers I used to get ten or fifteen years ago. And even when the answers are much the same, the reasons for giving them are different. It is not so much that the standard of virtue has been lowered to a level which almost disqualifies its claim to the title of virtue at all—and this has certainly come about in the case of a number of pretty jolly virtues— but rather that we tend nowadays to admire the virtues which we guiltily feel to be the opposite of our practice. That is to say we envy them; we don't aim at them. In- nocence appeals because, looking back, it is seen to have glamour. What seemed to have glamour *then*—when we were innocent—was sin. But sin was found to turn even glamour to ashes. In the abstract, academically, we still appreciate what is noble and fine and true . . . but of course it would be the most awful bore to pledge ourselves to its pursuit.

"We live by admiration." What Wordsworth meant by this was very different from what the phrase would convey at first sight to the average reader. The things that inspired his generation and urged it to feats of emulation bore ours to tears. The admiration we know is the kind we live *on* and not *by*. It is a brave man who can claim that his life is measured by his idealism. The most admirable is not always the most admired. Certainly it is admiration that is most envied. It feeds us. We need its stimulus. Fame is the spur. Glamour.

To distinguish between what is fine and what is flimsy requires no great powers of discernment; it is the decision to follow the fine in an age when flimsiness is the fashion that costs us dear. The trouble about the flimsy is that it never leads to anything lasting. It doesn't follow through. It delights but does not satisfy. So much does it delight sometimes that it can, after a while, be mistaken for satisfaction. Eventually the cream bun can be more easily digested than the roast beef. Not only our tastes but our capacities are subject to atrophy and readjustment. Therein lies the tragedy. This is the ultimate degradation—that we neither want nor value the good. St. Paul goes on and on about this, showing how "God delivers up to a reprobate sense those who will not have God in their knowledge".

Each new sin drives the soul farther along the way of maljudgement, guilty and deliberate.

Not only in individual souls does this rot set in, but in nations also. States, fed on creamy ideologies, have no stomach for Christianity. Glamour wins. The family, the school, the university—whatever unit you care to choose—that does not reject the idea of quick returns and get back to the principles of sound and not immediately rewarding work, is doomed to live unsatisfied, like a man on a diet of confectionery. Fortunately there will be a minority of those who are prepared to be hungry and lonely and unhappy and right, rather than be well off and popular and gay and wrong.

> This man is freed from servile bands
> Of hope to rise or fear to fall:
> Lord of himself, though not of lands,
> And having nothing, yet hath all.

How has it come about that the scheme of values is so different now from what it used to be? Why has not man seen through it all? The relentless quest for the superficial should long ago have brought its reaction. But not a bit. People wear themselves out over what does not matter with the same zest that wore out their fathers over what did. It has been well said of Jane Austen that she takes us into a forgotten world of comedy without footlights, conduct without crime, and love without sex. Why has this world been forgotten? Why do our nerves demand the glare of the footlights, and scream of crime, and the stink of sex? Why is Jane Austen's world a period piece? We can't lay all the blame upon the cinema. Hollywood may be responsible for a lot but it cannot have introduced a new morality into the world, an amorality without culture or rest or depths. The Industrial Revolution—that old chestnut—was it here that the trouble began? Democracy gone wrong? Material-ism? Possibly it is the result of many combined causes and trends, social and economic, artistic and philosophical, nationalistic and ideological. But whatever it is that has led men to look at the face instead of the heart it is only religion that can put man's vision right again. And for that he needs a new heart—let alone a new face. Look after the heart, and the expression will look after itself. Seek ye first the kingdom of God and all these things will be added to you. But for this we need the unbeglamoured eye of faith.

THE PRAYER-METHOD OBSESSION

PEOPLE imagine that they can never hope to be souls of prayer unless they become masters of one or other of the methods of prayer. Which, they say quite rightly, would mean learning up the thing, practising it according to the directions, consulting the authorities, probably even carrying a meditation book about with them to read in the train, making particular examens at odd times, and generally concentrating. "Really one has hardly got the time for it." The result is that the would-be aspirant to the prayer life confines himself for ordinary purposes to a handful of vocal prayers, and, as regards silent wordless prayer, attempts no more than occasional tip-and-run visits to the Blessed Sacrament. Let us examine this question of the necessity of prayer according to a method.

When the Psalmist prays "Show Lord, thy ways unto me", he is not asking God to show him some systems to choose from. In the Psalmist's time there were no systems apart from the very direct one of aspiring to be ever in the presence of the Lord. Which suggests that systematized prayer cannot be necessary to man, or God would not have allowed many hundreds of years B.C. and fifteen hundred years A.D. to go by without it. The faithful had somehow or other to get along as best they could. One can't help admitting that they managed very well.

At the same time that meditation books came in—during, that is, the same hundred years—there came in also for the rescue of fallen man such things as tobacco, tea, coffee, and (surprisingly) potatoes. It is hard to think of man doing without potatoes. But potatoes can't be necessary to him or it wouldn't have taken him all that time to dig them up. It is hard to think of a novitiate bookshelf without meditation books. But they can't be necessary or they would have been discovered sooner.

You might argue that potatoes, tea, and so on, are not strictly necessary, yet because they have replaced what were once necessities they can now be said to rank as such. The case is the same with regard to prayer: the older and more simple practice of directly seeking the presence of God has given place to what a great number of people feel to be a *necessary* form of the prayer expression. It should be remembered that systematized prayer is, like tea, a substitute. Is also, like tea, a stimulant. To change the metaphor, systematized prayer is a sort of mental crutch—something to lean upon when the limbs have not sufficient strength to propel the body on their own. In other words it is something to be discarded as soon as there *is* sufficient strength. And let it be noted that though we may lean on a crutch we do not learn to walk on one. The text-book is only something to fall back upon, not something to carry about.

One of the main drawbacks to the use of a text book is that we never know when to leave go of it. We begin to feel that without it we are not safe. It becomes a talisman, a superstition. Over-regulated mental prayer can fall into the same trap as over-elaborated ceremonial: the main business of prayer can be sacrificed to efficiency. By watching the progress of our minds through the various stages of the meditation we can forget all about God. We can become fascinated by the mechanism of it. It becomes an intellectual and not a spiritual exercise. The very rules which were designed to do away with distractions can themselves become a distraction. And when the time of prayer is over we shut the text-book with a snap and say,

"Well at any rate that must have been all right because I was doing something the whole time."

This, the sense that one has made one's contribution, we feel to be proof of the method's value. At last, unlike the blankness which resulted from the free wayless groping after God, here is a prayer which can show a return. Resolutions? Petitions? Acts of gratitude, remorse, resignation? Yes, there they are, lots of them, labelled correctly and tied together in neat little packets. It is gratifying to know that at least one is getting somewhere—it's not as if one was completely in the dark any more. But is this an assurance which we have any right to? Are we meant to be gratified by any such knowledge ? Isn't there the danger that we shall be praying in order to have these satisfactions and not in order simply to please God? Always we have to be reminding ourselves that we pray not in order to be good at prayer but in order to give God praise. The trouble about scientific prayer is that it is too good to be true. It produces, as a mechanical thing must, a lifeless article. It is too comprehensive. It doesn't leave room for either the individual or the Holy Spirit. Tidy and businesslike, it puts, as far as statistics go, the prayer of futility in the shade. But it does lay the soul open to the danger of complacency. Confidence in God and not in self is surely the first condition of true prayer.

To conclude: by no means let the crutch be despised provided it is really necessary. But crutches don't of themselves strengthen: in fact, if employed beyond the time of their usefulness, they actually weaken. The point of prayer is not to get one's dispositions tabulated but to direct one's energies towards their proper object—God. What they look like and feel like to us when they are engaged in this process does not matter in the least. God will straighten out that at His end. All we have to bother about is the act of love.

MORE ABOUT PRAYER

"IT IS VERY nice to be told that one's distractions don't destroy one's prayer," I was assured after a discussion of spiritual subjects, "but the fact remains that I simply do not pray." So I fell back upon the spiritual director's last line of defence and said: "Ah, you mustn't judge by the feelings."

But what else—let us admit it—has a man to judge by? It is a question which touches every department of the interior life (and a good many departments of the exterior life as well) so it is distinctly worth while trying to find an answer to it. "I'm presumably hot when I feel hot, I'm presumably in need of food, sleep, exercise and so on when I *feel* I want these things; what is there to tell me that my feelings, which apparently regulate my life and are to be trusted to decide whether I am in love, in health, in a temper, are to be written off the moment they start telling me about prayer?" Such an objection would be to the point if prayer were a physical activity conducted with purely natural organs, or even a mental activity restricted to the intellect alone, but prayer is neither. It engages the soul. It is converse with God. Grace—and not muscle or brain—is its medium. How can feelings possibly measure the success or failure of such an exercise? How can we, with our finite minds and values, form any sort of estimate of an effect the term of which is God? Indirect tests, yes, but certainly nothing so pulse-and-thermometer as whether or not the time of prayer went well. If there is one art or science or practice which defies the taking of degrees it is the spiritual life: we have nothing to examine it with. Plenty to examine it *on*, but nothing with. Save indirectly. There is only one person who can see exactly what is happening in our prayer, and that is God. The less we see of it the better. If we were practising prayer for our own benefit, or for the interest of our director, it would be a different thing. But we practise prayer for the purpose of pleasing God. And the answer is that provided we practise it we please Him—and if we don't we don't. Seen in those terms, it is obviously a waste of time to worry about what it feels like and how it can be made to feel better. What it feels like to God is the only thing that matters, and beyond the general knowledge that He is pleased by our effort we can never have the least idea as to what it feels like to Him. So there is no point in trying to find out.

Then what about these indirect tests? If I may not look at the prayer itself, what is there I can examine which will tell me that I am not on the wrong lines altogether? St. Teresa, by way of answer to this question, gives three signs which may be taken to show that the soul is in the right way of prayer. (But notice that she gives them for the use of the director rather than for the person who is looking for the satisfaction of security.) The signs are these:

First, courage in detachment—which means a process of weaning ourselves from the love of creatures. Not that we cease to see their beauty, but that we cease to depend upon their comfort. We come to see creatures in God, which is how we would have seen them without the least difficulty if there had been no fall. We come also to see God in creatures, where we would expect to find Him if we had not loved creatures first. "Courage in detachment" has a depressing ring about it, but it is not so depressing when we realize that it is our taste that has to undergo a change, not our capacity. From being attached to vanity, we become attached to reality. It needs courage certainly. But courage can be helped by common sense.

Second, zeal for souls—which means a growing desire for other people's perfection besides our own. If our prayer is going right—such is St. Teresa's view—we must inevitably want to give to others what we increasingly value as being the most important thing in the world. We hate to see people hiding from the light. We long that people should use their chances. We look more and more for the good which is hidden in the sinner. More and more we make allowances for the weak, the failures, the wrecks. We begin to feel the urgency of penance—not for ourselves merely, but for the world. Prayer teaches us all this.

Third, resignation under the cross—which is again a thing which prayer alone can teach us. Prayer *becomes* the cross. If we keep up the prayer, it becomes more than possible to become resigned to bearing it. Fidelity to prayer, moreover, leads progressively from shrug-shouldered resignation to acceptance, and from acceptance to voluntary oblation. The soul given to prayer comes to see that suffering not only fits in, but is the most appropriate expression of its love. It sees that however impenetrable the darkness the only thing is to go on and not to go back. The darkness is taken in its stride—as the most significant, though the most hidden, aspect of that cross to which prayer has taught it to be resigned.

When asked what he liked to see most in a House of Commons man, Disraeli said: "That he should be *there.*" The sign above all that one looks for in assessing the quality of a man's prayer is that he should *do* the thing. St. Teresa's tests are all very well, but if we are in a doubt about our

own prayer I wouldn't mind betting they help us hardly
at all. Dare I say that I'm getting more detached,
more apostolic, more resigned? I wonder. But I can
easily tell if I'm praying, or trying to pray, as much as
I used to.

THE PECULIAR ENCHANTMENT OF
MIDDLE AGE

O VER General MacArthur's desk hangs, I understand, the following reflexion: "Nobody grows old by merely living a certain number of years; people grow old by deserting their ideals. Years wrinkle the skin, but to give up enthusiasm wrinkles the soul."

It *is* true that the most ageing thing is ceasing to make the effort. Once a man says that it's not worth trying to live up to a standard he had set himself he has suffered a defeat more significant than being beaten in the ordinary way. To admit disillusion *is* being beaten: it allows that its estimate of the world's strength was wrong, and that the world has won. But there is no reason why we should allow this collapse to take place in middle age rather than at any other time.

What is it that prevents some people ever growing old? It is not that they preserve the manners of youth or that they have always had the knack of picking up the idiom of the moment. First and foremost it is their belief in young people, their willingness to understand, but really what underlies this sympathy is the fact that they have never ceased looking at life in the way that they did when they were eighteen. The qualities that characterized their youth were so strong in them that no amount of subsequent disappointment was able to have the slightest effect. In other words they went on the assumption that life was an adventure and that there were discoveries to be made round every corner. Most of us in middle life imagine that we have discovered years ago all that we are likely to

36

discover, and we settle down to a more or less flat enjoyment of the pleasures which experience has shown us to be within our scope. The vigour has gone out of us, there is no longer the expectancy of youth. What the young are looking for, says Disraeli rather sadly, is experience; and when they have got it they lack the energy to enjoy it. But surely you are as young as your hope, as young as your openness of heart. Youth can't be merely a question of energy and untried experience. It is much more a receptivity of mind, a courageousness of will, a confidence in life which can rise above such relatively artificial obstacles as health, years, and circumstances. It would be pleasant, of course, if we could continue through life as carefree and eager as we were before we grew up, but maturity has its compensations and the periods which follow youth need be no less vital, no less spirited. Unencumbered were the saints by their cares, as resilient at eighty as they had been at eight. The saints knew that they had something which no amount of wear and tear could spoil for them. "Neither death nor life nor angels nor principalities nor powers nor things present nor things to come nor might nor height nor depth, nor any other creature shall be able to separate me from the love of God which is in Christ Jesus." With such a confidence there need be no slowing down or falling off in middle age. In fact there is this about increasing years that one's experience of God and reality drive deeper, and that one's emotions somehow refine themselves and enlarge their capacity. There is a keener appreciation of even natural perfection where there is knowledge to go upon and previous discovery to be referred to. In the supernatural order this is still more the case. The mind that has kept untarnished its ideas of prayer, of love, of sacrifice, of the nobility that is in man, is richer at the age of fifty than at the age of twenty-five. With the accumulated wealth of faith it has no reason to envy the magnificence of the young. As long as we are only tamed by years and not tired by them we have no cause to worry. Nor should we suffer ourselves to be unduly tamed. Looking wide-eyed at life we shall find much that will create in us that blessed sense of wonder—so much indeed that there will be no room in us for preoccupation with the crooked and the wrong. "My dreams have been exploded long ago . . . I used to think like that once . . . when a man gets to my age . . . one has to be a realist after all." But idealism is real. It is seen to be more real on God's plane than on ours, but His is the true plane nevertheless. It is our faith that lets us see things as they really are. What men call the realistic view is more often the materialistic view; and the greater things of life which they have written off as un-attainable in this world come finally to be regarded as not worth attaining to in the next. Besides, even if we cannot get near to the heights, isn't it better to press towards them than to content ourselves with grubbing about in the valleys? Browning knew what he was talking about when he wrote:

A man's reach should exceed his grasp,
Or what's a Heaven for?

It's when we bring our Heaven down to earth and adjust it to the flat rate of our behaviour that we are becoming middle-aged. But not till then. Heaven will not be found in the bargain basement; we must live on the roof if we would see the sky.

THE PRAYER OF FUTILITY

THE GREAT complaint with most people about their prayer is that they never feel they're getting anywhere. But of course it would be a very bad sign if they did. A lot of the trouble about prayer would disappear if we only realized—*really* realized, and not just supposed that it was so—that we go to pray not because we love prayer but because we love God. Not in order to master distractions or perfect a system or because we have said we would go on with the thing, but simply in order to please God. Once granted that God's view of our prayer is the only one that is at all worth taking into account, it can't much matter what our own view of it is. In fact the less view we have of it— and for view we can substitute the word "feeling"—the better. This is what St. John of the Cross is talking about when he says that darkness in prayer is better than light. Better in the sense of being not only safer for us but making for a purer prayer in itself. This is a significant claim to make.

"Oh, I know all about that," you will say, "but it's no use telling me that God's way of judging prayer is so different from my way of judging it that what are distractions to me are praises to Him. Distractions and praises are not only different things altogether, they are completely opposite things. Your theory doesn't make sense." Excuse me, it does. In the first place the opposite to a praise is not a distraction but an insult—and ordinary distractions are certainly not that. In the next place we must remember that God's scale of values, His sphere of operation, His

39

terms, even, are quite different from ours. What is light
to Him is so luminous that to our materially focusing
eyes it appears as darkness. (This is not simply my idea:
it is St. John of the Cross' and, before him, Dionysius
the Areopagite's.) If we can't even look at the sun without seeing black spots everywhere, it is hardly likely
that we shall see very much of what we are looking
at when we are trying to train our gaze upon Light
Itself.

God knows the limitations which He has imposed upon
man and makes allowances: we think we can see ourselves
as God sees us and make difficulties. There *is* only one
test of our prayer: are we wanting God? Do we want
Him so much that we are prepared to go on looking for
Him in our prayer in spite of apparently never getting
any nearer to Him? Upon the answer to this enquiry
depends the whole business of our success or failure in
prayer. Success and failure to be judged in God's terms,
not ours.

The above may be easier to follow if we change the
approach. Take the Book of Job. Here we are granted an
intimate glimpse into the ways of God, the ways of the
devil, the ways of a certain holy man. First of all the devil
is briefed, by God's permission, for an attack upon the
man Job. Next the attack takes place. Then Satan returns
and presents his report. At first sight it looks a good report,
but by the time we have finished the Book of Job we
realize that the report can be pulled to pieces and that the
attack must have been a complete failure. The same sort
of thing is presumably still going on: the devil tempting,
God permitting, man resisting as best he can. There is
imperfection in the fight put up against temptation, and
sometimes it seems to the weary frightened soul that there
is nothing left of its resolve, but the struggle still goes on

and in the topmost pinnacle of the will there is still the refusal to be stampeded into evil. Our prayers, always by God's permission because He knows what is best for us, are for ever being invaded by dryness and distraction. The devil's reports are constantly coming in before the throne of God. There is the same misrepresentation. But though we may be deceived, God is not deceived. Pick out any day in our prayer life and consider the kind of account which Satan might present at the judgement seat of God. It shouldn't be a record of our resisting effort on a good day when perhaps we have been in form, but simply a frank statement of what has been going on when our prayer has run true to normal—when, in other words, it has been that boring blank, punctuated occasionally by the arrival of not very memorable diversions.

"See this dilapidated prayer," says the devil, "and tell me, Lord, whether You don't think it has been a waste of time. Those yawns, for instance, and those furtive glances at the watch—they must certainly score heavily in my favour. And what about that lengthy digression on the subject of his health? Then there was that argument which would have been so convincing if it had in fact taken place instead of being a fanned up piece of self justification existing only in the mind. And those plans for August. Followed by at least ten minutes when nothing seems to have gone on at all. Surely, Lord, You got very little out of that prayer to-day—especially if You take into consideration those memories and imaginations which I suggested to his muddy mind: memories which would be unsuitable anywhere but which are especially so at prayer. Even the attempts at returning to Your presence, Lord, can be counted as winning points to me: they were so half-hearted and infrequent. Add to the total that confessedly bored attitude of mind in which the whole thing was conducted and You will admit that I have won hands down."

So much for the devil's report. First of all there is nothing to show that our prayers are as boring to God as they feel to us. Moreover, even granted that in the given prayer there was nothing substantial which could be listed on the credit side (and there usually *is* something, though not always something you could put your finger on afterwards) it would surely be reasonable to think of God as countering Satan with the all-important question: "But whom was he doing it *for?*" *That's* the point. It would be in keeping with the spirit of the Book of Job to consider the Lord pursuing Satan relentlessly. "It's all very well for you to cite the distractions in My friend's prayer"—so we would have the Lord defending His own—"but though he may not have made a very good thing of it, at least he has not gone back to bed or picked up a novel. He did, you notice, *go on.* Discouraged as he is about the result of his effort (unreasonably discouraged in point of fact) he will be at it again, you will find, to-morrow morning. His object all along has been—and still is—to please Me, and though he imagines he isn't doing this, he has no intention of pleasing you. While certainly he isn't, poor man, pleasing himself."

The prayer of futility, then, has this inestimable advantage: it keeps us in our place. (It has its dangers too: particularly dejection and laziness.) It enables us to say with sincerity: "I am nothing. I can do nothing. I deserve nothing but kicks and crosses. At the same time nothing in the world will induce me to give it up." Such is the mind of the man of prayer. A fixed refusal to be put off by failure: a willingness to forgo the taste of success. The true soul of prayer strives after God alone. Not after satisfaction, not after recollection (for itself's sake), not even after sanctity (regarded as a state and not as a means of loving God), but simply after God Himself. And inevitably God is the reward of such a striving . . . but God expressing Himself more in His Absence than in His Presence. "You wouldn't be looking for Me," as He reassured Pascal, "if you hadn't already found Me."

THE ENGAGEMENT IS
ANNOUNCED . . .

THE TROUBLE about being engaged is that it bears very little relation to being married. Only in the widest sense is it a test: it is a prelude rather than a preparation to matrimony. The engagement period is often compared to the novitiate period in a religious order. This is a very poor analogy. Where the novice is shown the religious life in its least attractive aspects, the engaged couple show themselves necessarily at their best. Where the novice has a foretaste of the life's reality, the intended partners can only forecast the life in the imagination. Obviously it would be against the Catholic spirit to view marriage as the worldling professes to view it—as a gamble, a lottery, a chances-against-but-worth-experimenting affair—but it must nevertheless be, from its very nature, an act of faith.

"How can I be sure that this is the real thing?" Countless men and women have asked themselves the question. The answer is: You can't. That is you can't be absolutely sure, though there are indications which certainly help considerably in the decision. In the first place it is no use trying to determine the quality of your love by a process of comparison with your previous affairs of the heart. They all feel the same at the time, and if love is blind it is certainly blinding with regard to the past as well as to the present and the future. The act of falling in love is a new experience on each occasion, and every time it happens it has the inspiring effect of convincing the subject that now at least the authentic emotion has been evoked. Equally it is no use putting too much trust in one's estimate of what one will feel

44

like in five or ten years' time: one simply doesn't know. Besides, one's mental images tend to break down, when trying to anticipate them in the imagination, after the honeymoon. In other words the ground for investigation is neither the memory nor the imagination: both are dangerously fallible. The right conclusion is far more surely reached if I answer the far more realist questions: first, how do I regard the person concerned? second, what are my views of the contract itself?

Assuming that a man believes himself to be genuinely in love and not merely embarked upon a flirtation, he will find on examination that there are a number of by-products attaching to the dominant emotion which should be able to determine for him the general direction of the thing. First among such pointers would be the quality of respect—respect amounting almost to reverence. Do I (he can ask himself) so esteem my intended wife as to be able to use the word "honour" in the highest sense when it comes to the pronouncing of the vows? Because unless there is in the man this sense of delicacy towards the woman he intends to marry it is inevitable that the intimacies of married life will ultimately betray the sacramental character of the union.

Another such attitude or required approach is one which finds justification in that passage of the Book of Genesis which describes the original planning of the bond between man and wife. Before the coming of Eve we are told of Adam that "there was not found a helper like to himself". A helper. This, then, is to be one of the primary functions of the married man—he is there to help. In material needs obviously: in spiritual needs less obviously but no less really. God forbid that he should hinder, but positively he must *help* his partner on her way to God. And he in his turn must look to receive such assistance from her. He

must not resent—on the contrary he must welcome and
submit to—the reasonable exhortations of her whom God
has chosen from among thousands to further His interests
in this particular home. Support in the temporal order is
recognised as one of the chief concomitants long before the
man has brought himself to the point of proposing, but
how many people—bridal couples as they stand at the
altar on their wedding day—acknowledge that they owe
to God and to each other the duty of embarking upon a
hand-in-hand pilgrimage which ends only at the gates of
God's City? Yet unless there is this mutual confidence,
both in one's own desire to promote the other's progress
and in the other's willingness to profit by one's effort, there
is reason to doubt whether the contract is being undertaken
in any sort of supernatural spirit. Of that other, wider,
confidence between man and wife it is not necessary here
to speak. It is obvious. I mean the trust which dismisses
at once the suspicion born of gossip and jealousy, and which
is generous enough to treat lightly such lapses as are due to
frailty and not to settled infidelity. Without the cement
of trust the household will never survive the rot.

To take now the second point, the marriage contract itself, how does the would-be bridegroom view it? From the
Gospel standpoint or from that of Hollywood and the
divorce-court news? The first question in the Catechism
might be addressed equally to marriage as to man. And
receive the same answer. Who made marriage? Not the
State, not custom, not health considerations, but God.
"Matrimony" says the Catechism on a later page, "is the
sacrament which sanctifies the contract of the Christian
marriage." Which means that the union is simply what it
is in the sight of God. The sacramental quality is not something superimposed, an afterthought, an accidental which it
is nice for the pious to feel when their hands are joined in

holy wedlock: the sacramental quality is the basis of the whole thing or it is nothing. Not only does the Catholic put a supernatural orientation to his marriage but he sees, on the more strictly human plane, that the success of the venture depends upon nothing so much as upon the degree of the self-sacrifice which is reached by both parties. Sacrifice is the proper expression of love, and if one's love is found to be out for what it can get instead of for what it can give, its name is nearer lust than love: it is a parody of the real thing, a travesty. Newman says somewhere that unless the bond between man and woman is above nature it is hideously below.

"But if the case is as you say," it may, with the disciple in the Gospel, be objected, "then it were better not to marry at all." To which I answer: Yes, if you can't face those terms, much better. For unless you make of your marriage a wedding of what God wants wedded, and in the *way* God wants them wedded, you minister to yourself alone . . . and to the ultimate undoing of your married life.

THE DARK NIGHT OF HOPE

In these years after the second Germanic war and before we find ourselves involved in a different kind of war altogether it will be necessary to give especial emphasis to the virtue of hope. The attack on faith has been going on for twenty years and more: the Catholic has been told what to do about it. Charity is always being attacked—hatred of one's enemies is regarded as a patriotic necessity, hatred of one's friends as a pleasing affectation—and the Catholic is always being told what his duties are in this direction. But it is hope that has escaped attention—hope in God, in mankind, in our own interior lives, in ourselves.

St. Paul's symbol for hope is the anchor. He might have chosen the rising sun or the budding rose or the pearl within the oyster. Instead he chose the anchor. The reason for this is of course that the anchor represents stability, and it is the foundation of our hope rather than our hopeful feelings that the saint is all out to stress. Our hope, like our faith and our charity, rests on God's promises. If the virtue rested on the glowing sense of optimism which even in times of distress can still be elicited in the heart of man, the emblem would hardly have been an anchor. A fountain would have been more apt. But hope as a supernatural virtue has nothing to do with feelings of optimism. Or rather, we feel optimistic when we practise the virtue of hope, but we do not practise the virtue of hope because we feel optimistic. The grounds of our confidence are not a rosy future, a generous determination to put the best face upon the situation, a conviction that somehow or other things will right themselves as they always do: the grounds of our hope are not as variable. For us there is the absolutely solid assurance that whatever happens God has got the matter well in hand. Beyond that we need not worry. "The future holds out no hope whatever." What if, humanly speaking, it doesn't? "So-and-so is utterly hopeless." He isn't as far as God is concerned; if there were no more hope for So-and-so, he would not be allowed to go on. "I feel the spiritual life is so hopeless in my case." It isn't, or God wouldn't have wanted you to live it. "I've given up all hope." Ah, if that is true, then indeed there has been an apostasy: it is the same as saying that you have given up faith, that you have given up charity. The moment a man gives up hope—really gives it up, not merely sinks for a time under the weight of depression—he has committed the sin of despair. Despair is the sin which cannot find—because it will not look for it —forgiveness.

Perhaps because the dark night of hope has come down upon a world that has been shaken out of its wits by the discovery of the atom bomb, men are looking into their own souls for the securities which they know they will never find in the outside world. There is this to be said for dissatisfaction, that if we despair of the wrong things we may begin to value the right ones. Until a soul realizes that there are some things which no dictator, no political system, no weapon of destruction can take from him, he will never know the reality of hope. It is not the saints alone who must place their happiness out of reach from human recall: we must all do it. St. Paul's anchor has this peculiar quality about it that it has to be thrown up into the heavens and not down into the depths. Our anchorage finds no sure hold in this world, and once it is firmly locked in the confidence which is assured us by faith there is no storm that can break the chain. We shall be tossed about, we shall be deafened by the roar, we shall doubt if there will ever come a dawn, but if we are anchored to our hope in God's promise we have nothing to fear.

In our personal relationship with God in prayer it is more often a want of hope than a want of faith that causes us to weaken. It is not that we despair of ultimate salvation but that we get discouraged at the present lack of result. Discouragement breeds listlessness. "What's the use?" "I'll never conquer this sin." At the outset we must be fully determined to hold out against two most disrupting fallacies: one, that it's not worth while going on with a serious purpose of prayer, and two, that any sin is ineradicable. We must treat these feelings of hopelessness as we would treat any other spasms: we must not allow ourselves to be stampeded. It is easier to recognize over-confidence—which is also an attack against the virtue of hope—as a mood. We know from previous experience that we shall soon slide back into our more normal self-distrust. But even our self-distrust (if it is the wrong kind of self-distrust) is to be taken as a mood, and mistrusted accordingly. All extremes of feeling are to be held suspect. They make for unreality. But especially are we to cultivate the serenity and detachment of the saints with regard to temptations of presumption and despair.

We ask, as we always ask when we are tempted to anything, why does God allow it? And the answer is always the same: if we could be *sure* of ourselves we would cease to trust in God. That would be presumption. But God doesn't want us to stand secure on our own feet without reference to Him. He allows us to panic so that we should turn to Him. In the dark night of hope we turn to Him in the same way that we turn to Him in the dark night of faith: we stay still, shutting our eyes to false dawns, abandoning ourselves without reflexions and examinations into His hands. Not looking for reasons, not making decisions, not dramatizing our distress, we simply wait for the trial to pass. There will be, just as there will be in the dark night of faith, great loneliness and perhaps great melancholy, but the darkness will be shot through from time to time by shafts of light.

The feelings of hopelessness which with the best will in the world we are powerless to resist are all part of the process whereby God would have us purify every faculty, interior as well as outward. We are not responsible for our faculties, but we are responsible for the exercise of our wills, and if our wills are united to His will He can be left to exercise our faculties as He chooses. We are like patients in hospital: not responsible for our temperatures but able to make decisions as to whether we wish to be moved. We decide only to be moved if God wills it. "The Lord ruleth me and I shall want for nothing." This is the verse of hope. Not looking for a solution in creatures, not allowing ourselves the spurious luxury of cynicism, not rebellious or impatient against the Providence of God . . . such is the hope of the saints.

> And if I stoop
> Into a dark tremendous sea of cloud,
> It is but for a time: I press God's lamp
> Close to my breast: its splendour soon or late
> Will pierce the gloom: I shall emerge one day.

Until that day dawn—and it may not dawn at all while I am in this mortal flesh—I shall go on hoping. Hope deferred is good enough for me. And that I should be able to say this is perhaps the purpose of the whole thing.

THE DARK NIGHT OF CHARITY

IF THE virtues of faith and hope have to endure obscurities, it is not surprising that the greatest of the theological virtues, charity, should also have to go through its time of trial. If charity covers a multitude of sins, it is obviously in the devil's interest to make that multitude of sins look as if it was covering charity.

Taking first the charity which we owe to God, we can apply the same rules and tests which are applied to the nights of faith and hope. Just as faith means clinging on when we feel we have nothing to cling on to, and hope means looking forward when we seem to have nothing to look forward to, so love means being faithful when everything seems to point to the uselessness of our fidelity. And it means more than this. By the dark night of charity is meant that state of soul wherein bitterness struggles for the place which is felt to have been abandoned by God. God seems to have lost interest; the service which we render Him is without zest; the whole meaning of the word "love" as applied to the relationship between the soul and God, whatever meaning it had in the beginning, is felt to be a mockery. Not only has devotion, such as we conceive it to be, fled from us, but so have the gift of piety, the interest which we felt at one time in the Church, our zeal for the liturgy, and in fact all the expressions of our love of God . . . they have all gone. That is what I mean by the dark night of charity. But like the other nights it has no real foundation: it is only a glorified nightmare. Oh yes, it is meant by God to take place, and in that sense it is very real indeed. It is real also in that it plays a necessary part in the development of the soul's perfection. All I am saying is that the grounds for fear—and it is fear that causes the pain of this night—are without substance. In other words that the soul is really loving God the whole time only it doesn't know it.

Prove it, you will say. I can't. But apply the tests and you will soon—in the case of judging other people anyway —have all the assurance you want. However much the soul feels the uselessness of trying to love God, does it still continue to try? Does it go on with love's acts? Does it speak the language of love, is it willing to sacrifice, long after the feeling has been borne in upon it that its words are not of the slightest interest and that its offerings are not looked at? If the soul goes on in the teeth of these misgivings, if it still wants to serve God even though God appears not to want its service, if it sticks to the original programme not because it is a programme but because when it was originally conceived it had about it the stamp of authenticity, then surely the quality of that love is proved. What more can the soul do? And if sacrifice is the stuff of love's expression, then this, the sacrifice of knowing that there is a response to one's love, is the offering of what is the most fundamental in human nature. Of course the word "love" changes as we live it: it does even in human affairs. But because it becomes less perceptible by the senses it is not on that account any less deep. Rather the reverse. The love between man and wife which has stood the test of thirty years is a more real thing now than it was at the time of the engagement. There may be no thrill about it, but if generosity and fidelity and unselfishness are the qualities of true love then the thing is as true as it is meant to be. The case for divine love is precisely the same. And if in the loneliness of feeling that it neither loves God nor is loved in return, the soul asks what is to be *done*, there is but one answer: go on. No looking back to happier times, no straining the heart to feel a devotion to which it cannot here and now pretend, no artificialities, no reserves. "Do I want God?" is the only test, and not "Do I feel I want Him?"

Our Charity towards man can also share this dark night of apparent eclipse. We long to escape the company of even those whom we like, let alone those whom we dislike. We know at the same time that this disgust is unreasonable and that we are to blame for what we apparently cannot help. And this very fact makes us worse. Then we start looking about for excuses to justify our attitude: we plead our temperament, our health, our age, our work—anything that will satisfy our consciences and tell us that we can leave others well alone. Sometimes we even tell ourselves that our call to solitary prayer is such that we can afford to cut ourselves off from the common herd. The call for this would have to be very clear indeed.

Certainly this malaise *may* be due to uncharity, but if a soul is given to prayer and has no reason to reproach itself for deliberately turning away from the love of its fellow men, then there is reasonable ground for believing that the whole thing is a trial—either sent by God as part of the positive process of spiritual formation or else allowed by Him as a temptation to be overcome like any other. Again what are the tests? By their fruits shall the tree be known. If irritation, dismissive manners, criticism, a censorious and self-opinionated attitude towards others are the only evidences to go by then obviously we have got the whole thing wrong. But if we honestly make ourselves as accessible, sympathetic, welcoming and joyous with others as we ever did when we felt well disposed towards them we have no reason to fear that we are losing the most precious of virtues. But can we always decide? Are we not too close up against ourselves to see? Back, then, to the test with which we tried out the quality of our love of God: do we *want* to love our neighbour? "Oh yes, in *theory* my zeal for souls is as good as it ever was . . . but it's in theory only, and even then when it's narrowed down to a single soul, I'm not at all sure . . ." Aren't you? Wouldn't you walk across Europe barefoot to prevent a soul committing sin? Are you really so indifferent to other people's salvation as you think you are? These individuals whom you shrink from when you see them coming, would you really not go to almost any lengths to make them happy if you could—let alone holy? Extend the test further. What happens in your heart when you read of the spread of obscene literature, when you hear of the apostasies of priests, when you see a boy getting drunk or hear a girl blaspheme? Is it that you are merely shocked when you come across these things? Isn't it rather that your whole being is saddened, that you feel it as a waste of Christ's Passion, as a positive wound? And on the other side, is there not a tremendous joy inside you when you watch innocence being preserved, and a sinner getting on top of his sin? These, and not the other, are the indications as to whether you have or have not lost your charity. The fact that your surface self shrinks from association with others is nothing to go by. A man with a tender skin draws away instinctively from the heat of a fire: it is not that he condemns fires or despises warmth but simply that for the time being it hurts him to expose the part of him that is sore and over-sensitive. The roughness will wear off, and in the meantime he gets as near to the glow as he can.

In the night of charity the treatment is as before: patience, gentleness, trust. Greater love than this no man hath, than that he should lay down his life for his brother. At no time more surely than in the night does a man lay down his life for love. If we have the generosity to offer, in the will, our lives for our brethren, we can well afford to do without the satisfaction, in the feelings of having offered.

LONELINESS

LONELINESS takes many forms, all of them quite frightful. There is a natural loneliness and a spiritual loneliness: the former is more poignant, the latter more searching. Some think that there is a cure for natural loneliness. There isn't. Time is a remedy but not a cure; it will reappear again. You can treat it with the remedies for spiritual loneliness, but even then you cannot be sure that you will get what you want—the reason being that you are probably wanting the wrong thing; which is probably why you are lonely. (These obscure remarks will straighten out as the essay proceeds.) Of spiritual loneliness there is no need to write here. The sense of being left alone by God, and the general desolation of thinking that He doesn't care, have been dealt with elsewhere in this book.

After sin, the three evils most to be dreaded are doubt, fear and loneliness. Of these, loneliness is the worst. Loneliness can give rise to doubt and fear, while if a man knows that he is not alone he can fight his doubt, and disguise—which is half the battle—his fear. We can force ourselves to laugh at our doubts and fears, but loneliness forbids laughter. Loneliness is an echoing ache in the soul, it hollows out the heart and scoops away at our reserves. It even communicates itself to the senses, and all the outer world seems indifferent and even hostile. We must have something with which to meet this evil. We must find something which will turn it into a good.

There is the loneliness of being in a strange place, of isolation; there is the more subtle loneliness which comes upon one in a crowd; there is the unreasonable loneliness which sometimes follows the closing of a door; there is the still more unreasonable loneliness which quite unaccountably grips the heart at times when all should be going well. Perhaps different temperaments suffer different spasms, so the best way to treat this subject is to take it in its most general form as the mood which is occasioned by the wrench of parting. For the settled melancholy which is not a mood but a habit of mind—the grim loneliness of old age for instance, or the mental isolation which is experienced by those in high office—the solution is the same. But it will be of the recurring rather than of the permanent loneliness that we shall be thinking in these paragraphs.

We feel lonely when people go away. Part of ourselves goes with them, and the resulting emptiness is like losing a limb. It is as if a mental leg had been cut off: there has to be a period of time before the one remaining leg can do the work of two; for a while the balance has been upset; the state is not normal. In the interval the whole horizon is darkened; the familiar world sighs at the absence; nothing seems real or worth while; there is the sense of finality—not absolute finality which would be a relief but the finality of feeling that there is nothing to look forward to but a dreary succession of years with their dreary succession of now lifeless tasks.

> Gone the sparkling days of June,
>   The radiance of July . . .
> All faded in an afternoon:
>   They died . . . and so did I.

This is where we need to have faith. This is where we pull ourselves up and cry "It's a mood. It will pass. It is only a mood." That *désespoir des lendemains de fête* will melt away in time, giving place to colour and light and normality and, finally, joy. That is the way of it. Life has to be so or it would be insupportable. But note that loneliness is not simply a matter of feeling flat after a time of happiness. It is not just anti-climax; not just a pang at seeing the crib figures put away till next year or hearing the cold tea being emptied onto the flower beds after a party. It is something much more real than mere wistful retrospection. It has a lot to do, of course, with nostalgia, but it is essentially a positive and not a negative hell. It is not simply doing without a companionship—though that is the main thing— it is the feeling that one has now to face life without the equipment which is due.

Like other moods, loneliness seems to set up a barrier which separates a man from his fellow men. A film comes in between, and the one thing which could ease his suffering is, by the very suffering, kept at arm's length. He has nothing but his memories to associate with, and these are the worst thing for him. "God gave us memory that we might have roses in December", but for him in his present mood the petals have fallen and he has only the thorns. The sky, the trees, his room, the routine of his day, the hundred unnoticed objects which surround him speak to him of an absence which again is a positive and not a negative thing. It is easier to escape from a presence than from an absence. Added to the sense of loss is often the sense of waste, and when these two go together, a man's lot is very hard indeed. Quite frankly I am amazed at how, without religion, such a state of mind can be endured. Why there are not more suicides I cannot imagine.

But *with* religion the whole thing adds up. Given a belief in an abiding city not made with hands of which we in this world are citizens-elect, there is something to look forward to. Granted friendship with One who in His loneliness cried "Why hast thou forsaken me?" we are never completely alone. Accepting the doctrine of the Cross we see our suffering as part of a pattern, woven into the tapestry not on a single thread but inseparably with His, and dyed in the same dye.

The soul hardly ever realizes it, but, whether he is a believer or not, his loneliness is really a homesickness for God. The sense of loss and emptiness does not derive from being away from this or that person, this or that place, but from being away from God. What has happened is that the soul has made for itself, out of a person or a number of persons or a place, what it thinks to be a home. But man is an exile on this earth, and when he is parted from these self-made homes he is like a lost sheep. Until he has found his permanent place in God he is bound to feel more or less lonely—out of place—in the world. It isn't wrong for man to try and find in people and places a temporary home. In fact it is what he is meant to do. But he must realise that it is temporary, that's all, and that people aren't God. He must never completely settle down. And because he may never do this, God sees to it that he is uprooted from time to time and parted from those he loves, so that in the sadness which follows he may remember that he is but a pilgrim and a stranger upon the earth and that it will be time enough later on to settle down and live happily ever afterwards. If our homesickness teaches us where to look for what we want, it will not have been suffered in vain. And though in this life we may never enjoy permanent companionship in fact, we most certainly can in faith. We have the presence of Christ to resort to in the tabernacle, and with Holy Communion every morning we need never feel entirely on our own. A priest once told me that except for the time when he was saying Mass he felt a complete misfit all day long. He was not, I think, a lonely man, but without the home which he held between his fingers every day at the altar he would have been.

So loneliness is at once a blessing and a curse: a curse, because it not only hurts but can spoil us; a blessing because it leads to the companionship of Christ. Like so much else in life, it is just what we make of it. It can so weigh us down that we become listless, unstable, sentimental—half the sloppy songs in existence are about it—isolationist, self-pitying on the one hand, and greedy for compensating satisfactions on the other. Whereas looking at it in its promising aspect, it can purify our natures to the extent of making us far less hard in dealing with others, far more sensitive to the calls of grace and true friendship. It is astonishing how much, both of good and evil, can be traced to loneliness of spirit. Ruthless ambition is often a craving to find what a temporary home—in the sense discussed—has failed to provide; lust is only the perverted hunger for companionship; jealousy is simply an inordinate fear lest the love which alone is felt to be capable of staving off loneliness be given to another. St. Thomas says that all sin is the mistaking of the means for the end. Loneliness is the price we pay for stopping short at creatures. But it is not easy to wait all our lives for the Creator. Sometimes our loneliness is in the nature of things; but sometimes it is due to sin. There is no loneliness like the loneliness of sin. Hell is no more than that after all: the pain of loss—guilty loss. The absence of love—wasted love. The great sinners of history, from Judas downwards, have been lonely men. So have the great saints. The Psalmist was a desperately lonely man—that is why we find in his verses a consolation which no other writing can give. But where the sinners began and ended lonely, the saints only began so. Once taken to heart the words "I am with you always, even unto the consummation of the world", there can be no more real loneliness. "If any man thirst, let him come to me and drink." For those who can take it, that is the answer.

THE EMOTIONS

W HEN TWO doctors of the Church are found to disagree
it is a heaven-sent opportunity for the ordinary hack like
myself to plunge in and express an opinion. St. Augustine
is down on the emotions, saying that their only function is
to stir the soul to action, and that if they fail in this they had
better be suppressed altogether. St. Thomas (who of
course was a far less emotional person than St. Augustine)
is rather for the emotions, saying that their expression relieves
the sensitive faculties of the soul of their superfluities. All
this is comforting because it means that if you are crying
madly at a cinema you can say to yourself: "St. Thomas
would approve of this: the soul is being purged of superficial sentiment." Whereas if you are surrounded by
weeping cinema-goers while remaining yourself unmoved
you can say: "Look at these weaklings . . . not a sign of
their being stirred to action . . . what would St. Augustine
say?"

Perhaps the truth is that you cannot generalize about the
emotions because they operate differently in different people.
It is a question of temperament, and if there is one thing
about which psychologists are agreed it is that certain
natures respond to a whole range of stimuli which may mean
little or nothing to others. That which may have stirred
St. Augustine to action may have stirred St. Thomas merely
to tears. No blame to St. Thomas: the two men were made
differently.

The practical problem arises as to how to deal with our
particular natures: each one's emotional system has to be

trained in the right direction and safeguarded from the wrong influences. It is not the least use denying the existence of our emotions—to do so would be just as superficial as to exploit and parade them—nor is it possible to destroy them out of hand. We control the emotions by refusing to be subject to our moods. "My soul is in my hand always" says the Psalmist. He had his emotions in order. Just as the sense of humour can degenerate into buffoonery, so the nobler senses, the emotions, can stray into sentimentality. There must be an austerity about our emotions as there must be an austerity about our bodies. More easily prostituted than any other is the emotion of love; but love is not the only emotion. Fine emotions can be cheapened, and cheap emotions can be refined, but no emotions can be, with safety, wallowed in. To wallow is to mistake the means for the end. This is what St. Augustine was talking about. Once we wallow we reduce the whole noble range of powers to a vulgar collection of luxury sensations. Joy becomes frivolous, sorrow grows mawkish, our affections get messy, and our loftiest enthusiasms are larded over with silliness.

Are we, then, never to indulge our emotions? Is there no occasion when, with the careless abandon which we remember from the halcyon days before we took up the spiritual life, we may let ourselves go? By way of answer let us split the emotions and put them on two levels. (Which is what St. Thomas did.) There are the deeper emotions—theologians call them passions—and there is the top-soil stuff. It is not that they differ in kind, they differ merely in degree. It is the deeper level that we have to take care about: what is on the surface we must learn to laugh at. An emotional man is not necessarily one who shows his feelings, whose heart is on his sleeve. An emotional man is simply a man of acute sensibility: if this comes much to the surface he is a superficial man. It is therefore our business to keep the emotions well down. At times they will work upon us so powerfully that we shall feel our anchorages to be giving way. We shall be—to use the stock phrase—profoundly moved. It is then that we shall need the strength which the life of grace has built up. It is then that our characters are tested. It is then, and perhaps even more when the emotion has spent itself and we are in the state of reaction and nervous exhaustion afterwards, that we need to have reserves to draw upon—interests of one kind or another. Emotional people are all too seldom told how vital it is for them to cultivate an intellectual background: they cannot, and should not, live in the emotions, and if they have nothing to fall back upon when the emotions dry up they will find themselves at the mercy of suicidal depressions which tend to drag on until the next emotional upheaval takes place.

As regards passing moods of ecstasy and agony, the thing to do is to take them for what they are worth and not to be either greedy for their pleasures or beaten down by their pains. Knowing the instability of our temperaments we must allow for the swing of the pendulum. Let us face it: there will be days when we shall think we are beyond the reach of depression for ever, and there will be days which we shall spend miserably longing for even the temporary solace of sleep. But nothing stays the same: life moves on. We can never hold on to the moments of happiness and we can never leapfrog the moments of gloom. Sunshine is meant to be taken as sunshine, and not as eternal light. We may not pick up our patches of sunshine in the hope that we shall have something to console us in the darkness of the night. Happiness is too big a thing for that. We can't enjoy it all at once; it has to be spread out. The experience of happiness is progressive, and may not be crystallized. "Let us build here three tabernacles", is a wish which is instinctive, but it isn't one which allows of satisfaction. We are given the faculty of remembering, and this is quite enough to go on with in this life. Indeed a happiness grows, matures, takes on new colour as it is remembered. We make the mistake of thinking that happiness can be a static thing, that we must squeeze every drop out of it while it is there or we shall miss it, that it is over and done with when we look back at it. Real happiness stands outside time, it is part of eternity. Memory is not an instrument, a sort of looking glass, for reflecting a past joy. It is not a sort of gramophone for recording a dead melody. Memory is part of the joy, it is an extension of happiness itself. The glory that is forgotten was no glory. The moment of happiness that we look back upon with pleasure was only the beginning: the happiness itself is not finished yet. Surely this should prevent us from being grasping? Surely this should let us take our moods of exaltation in our stride? And the other moods, those that plunge us into the depths, are to be thought of in the same way. They cannot, may not, last. Sadness never represents the real man for any length of time because it is more in the nature of man to be happy than to be miserable. Grief can be agonizing in its intensity: it can reduce a soul to bitterness, to sin, to madness, even to death; but it can never so overwhelm a man's spirit as to involve him in a settled unhappiness unless he deliberately indulges it. There is the danger: hugging one's sorrow until it becomes part of oneself. Thus, as long as we have the sense to take our moods of misery as moods, we are in no real danger of falling into a self-pitying decline. Our glooms need never reveal our real selves; they are more often physical reactions than natural tendencies.

To conclude, we can say with St. Thomas that our emotions—even when they express themselves in moods—

have their place in the general make-up of man and are on that account not to be despised. Like everything else in the make-up of man they are to be handed back to God as part of the humanity that He has redeemed. Emotions, like any other talents, are to be trained. The training and direction will require delicate handling, but to imagine that they can safely be screwed down under a lid is to miss the whole point. Besides, they will, if subjected to such a treatment, blow up. And nothing could be more dangerous than that. Whatever is wrong about the emotions has to be outplayed by whatever is right. The cockle *can* spoil the growth of the wheat, but it is no solution to the main problem to concentrate on the cockle. Look after the wheat and the tares will look after themselves.

COMPASSION

PERHAPS we have done enough about the emotions. There is however something to be said about one particular emotion, sympathy, and the place to say it is immediately after the foregoing essay.

We are inclined to think that passion—in the sense of suffering, not in the sense of rage or desire—is the main thing and that compassion is a sort of poor relation. If it is only this and not a co-suffering, if it is not a sympathy that shares, if it is not a willingness to bear at least an equal part if not a greater part or indeed the whole of the burden, then it isn't compassion at all but merely pity. We can feel pity at a cinema or over a novel. Compassion is reserved for reality. Possibly there are some people who have never experienced the emotion of compassion; if there are it must mean that they are either very selfish or very unreal. Compassion makes people real; makes them, for the time at least, unselfish. That is the whole point. That is why as an emotion it is of the highest quality. It takes a man away from himself and sinks him in the sufferings of others. Not all the emotions are virtues, but compassion can hardly help being one. Not all emotional people are good, but all good people—really good people anyway—are compassionate. They can hardly help it. Even quite ordinary people are raised to a level of goodness which is not normally theirs when practising the virtue of compassion. Even in fallen man compassion is instinctive; by grace and effort it can become the most blessed of virtues.

We have seen on a previous page that happiness is not finished when the occasion of the happiness is over. Sorrow is not isolated either. It is not strictly localized, incommunicable, complete in itself. If a sadness were simply like a wound—a hurt suffered on a single skin—then there would hardly be room for more than pity. "I am sorry for you, it looks terribly painful." That is all we could say. But sadness is not like that; it is a hurt that can be entered into by someone else. Sorrow, and even the suffering that sheer physical pain gives rise to, can be endured by another as if it were his own. Such is the way of things among human beings that, whether the suffering of one member is physical, mental, moral, or spiritual, there is an answering spark that can be kindled in the souls of other members. Whether or not the flame can bring consolation to the original sufferer, it can certainly sear the soul of the one who brings compassion. So deeply can some natures feel the miseries of others that often the elicited sorrow is more agonizing than the evil which causes it. A man may suffer more over a friend's distress than the friend does, and certainly he suffers more than if the distress had happened to himself. We all, in some degree, experience this. We can be made much more wretched by having to stand by and witness the grief of someone we care for than we would be if we could substitute ourselves instead. It is the inability to help that causes the poignancy of compassion's grief. We feel that if the thing were happening to us alone we could help ourselves, or else do without help altogether, but because it is happening to someone else and because we can't be of any practical use we feel frustrated and miserable. Much as our own temptations may worry us, we can be driven almost desperate with anxiety over the thought of another being tempted in the same way. This is a puzzling fact, and though there may be much imperfection in it, the underlying instinct is surely a right one: it is the instinct to keep holy what is good—whether it happens to be in us or in anybody else. The fact that it is a good which is in someone else is no bad sign: it is better to worry over other people's worries than to worry over our own. There is no agony in the world like the agony of having to watch a dreadful thing going on in another, the course of which we are unable to control or even influence. Human patience is not big enough to cope with this; it is a thing which requires the highest confidence in God. But whether it is over a sin or a sickness, a disillusion or a defeat, the fact of having to play the part of passive spectator to another's drama is an experience so purifying that fortunate are they who have been given the grace to endure it. They will never be quite the same again.

Raise all this to the supernatural level and you see at once what were the emotions of the saints when they contemplated the sufferings of our Lord. Here is true compassion in its purest form. Longing to be of use, longing to bear something of the shame, longing to relieve the pain, longing to express the sympathy which is there but which can find no outlet. Helpless looking on. Helpless? No, not so helpless. The desire to help *is* help.

Of all Mary's titles, that of our Lady of Compassion is surely the noblest. In the light of Mary's seven sorrows it would surely be impossible to claim that the emotions, when not translated into act and when not positively effectual, were to be frowned upon.

To conclude. If it is true that "whatever excellence a man hath is his for the benefit of his fellow men", then it is also true that whatever better feelings a man may have he must extend for the consolation of others. And you couldn't have a better feeling than compassion. It is our compassion that is asked for in the heartrending reproaches of Good Friday. It is our compassion that is asked for by the Psalmist when he says in the person of Christ: "I looked for one that would grieve together with me but there was none; and for one that would comfort me but I found none." When we grieve together with the members of Christ's Mystical Body we grieve with Him; when we comfort them we comfort Him. That is what our emotions are for—to be used for other people. But used wisely. We may not parade our emotions—even sympathy can become sticky and tiresome when overdone—but the more altruistic they become, the better. The more lively of our emotions are to be used for jollying up other people, the deeper ones for bringing them what we have to offer. But as always in this business of human relationship there are dangers to be avoided: nothing is ever as forthright as it looks. The particular danger here is the *playing* upon the emotions of others. Few things are more degrading than to make capital out of other people's feelings. Most degrading of all of course is to do so by exposing our own.

BUILDING DUNGEONS IN THE AIR

I⟨T⟩ is not that at any time we deliberately choose depression in preference to joy, or that we consent to become cynics instead of deciding to be idealists, it is simply that we drift along until we find when we look into it that our normal mood is one of depression, that our outlook is that of the cynic. Imperceptibly the difficulties of life have hollowed out for us a sort of rut, and we have never had the energy or the enterprise to jump out of it. It is when we have woken up to the fact that we are rutted and *then* make no effort to alter the situation that the real failure begins.

At what stage in a man's life does all this begin to declare itself? Certainly people aren't, whatever you may say, born pessimists. Nor is pessimism, as greatness is with some, thrust upon them. Therefore they acquire it. But when? And how? And in heaven's name why? As a child no one is pessimistic or cynical: the embittered infant would be a monstrosity. In boyhood there is a lot of grumbling but there isn't much settled resentment, not much that is blighted and casts a blight. The thing seems to manifest itself most often in early manhood, when a pose of some sort is found to be convenient, and the most convenient pose is found to be cynicism. Take the case of the average young man who is making discoveries in literature and who is going frequently to the play. The epigram dazzles him; he is enchanted by the witchery of Oscar Wilde, of Bernard Shaw, of Noel Coward. Consciously or unconsciously his manner is affected by the models he finds in front of him. Where he fails to assimilate the good and the essential about the authorities whom he studies, he finds it easy enough to echo the lighter and more accidental elements. What the literary neophite sees in his favourite authors is the attention-value of these destructive scintillations, what he does not see is the lighthearted spirit in which such cynicism is conceived. He has yet to learn that most successful playwrights are born with a silver tongue in their cheeks.

If you are going to put on an act at all you will find that mockery is the easiest one to play. (Unless of course you play the pathetic, but this will be found to pall after a while.) Mockery may be the criticism of the insensitive but at least it is good for a certain amount of applause. There are so many things which lend themselves to facile ridicule, and from gayly scoffing at enthusiasm, patriotism, earnestness and so on it is the easiest thing in the world to slide into the habit of deriding fidelity, sincerity, purity, prayer and the Christian values generally. Long after the other affectations which one picks up in youth have been dropped, the affectation of cynicism is found to persevere. Provided it is an affectation, and recognized as such by the person himself and everyone else, it doesn't matter much, but affectations have a way of becoming part of one. They are one's second nature. And eventually not even one's second.

Youth gives place to middle age, and the jaundiced outlook, if it isn't thrown off by that time, is ingrained. Nothing is right; nothing is worth striving for. Where before one laughed at everything that was worth while now one groans at everything whether it is worth while or not. "He's like that; you shouldn't take him too seriously." But every now and again he *is* taken too seriously and the result is bad. Middle age gives place to riper years, and at a time when a man is in a position to advise others from the fruit of a lifetime's experience he has nothing to offer but a resentful retrospect. "The old boy's embittered; don't listen to him." Heavens, what opportunities lost! All this presents a gloomy picture; but then bitterness and pessimism make up a very gloomy disease. Fortunately it is a disease that may be cured. There is no one in the world so happy as the converted cynic. If only those know hope who have tasted of despair, then possibly it is only those who have come through their bitterness who can value what it is to be free of it, and measure the danger of its poison. Certainly where there is bitterness there can be no sort of sanctity. There can be few saints who have spent much of their time being sad, but there can be none at all who have spent much of their time being sour. Yet it is something which nearly everyone experiences for a time. Fortunate if it is only for a time. Sorrow can reduce us for a while, but if we indulge our sorrow it can become the weakness of a lifetime. Even resentment, so long as it is a spasm and not a fostered grudge, is natural enough—we can no more help being hurt by the sting of malice than by the sting of a bee—it is when it becomes a drawn out quarrel with existence, it is when we find ourselves at variance with life that we need to take ourselves in hand. Affliction, however persistent, should have no power to sadden. "We suffer tribulation but are not distressed," says St. Paul, "we are straitened but are not destitute, we endure persecution but are not forsaken, we are cast down but we perish not." Cast down often, but never so prostrate that we may not rise and go on. Grief, yes, but never a grievance. If we fail to master our moods, our moods will master us. There is no more masterful mood than that of bitterness, and fallen nature meets it more than half-way. But grace is stronger than fallen nature, and there is no reason why there should not be, even in the weakest of us, that rock-constant quality which a friend would call single-minded idealism and an enemy obstinacy. Indeed, unless we are so orientated I do not see how we can expect to be the slightest use in the world. Without such a flaming hope to keep us up to standard, we inevitably sink to the level of the disillusioned. Perhaps it wouldn't matter so much if man could keep his disillusion to himself, but there is in him always the tendency to infect others. If charity, love, is catching, so also is the want of it. Insufficiency of love is at the root of all cynicism, and this insufficiency drains the energy out of others. Cynicism can be as subversive as any sin. I have seen more wreckage done among the innocent by the man who sneers at virtue than by the man who solicits to vice.

THE MISSING LINK

I ONCE had occasion to visit a convent school on some preaching or lecturing engagement, and having disposed of my obligations I thought I had better call on the Reverend Mother. I was duly shown into a parlour and asked to wait: Reverend Mother wouldn't be a minute. On the table, next to a noble brass pot of maidenhair fern, were two albums containing scraps. Idly, the way one does when waiting for someone who won't be a minute, I turned the pages. There were views of Venice (those familiar views of Venice), Christmas cards, reproductions of the masters, pictures of birds, fruit, nuns, uniforms, flowers, more nuns, Scotland, a bishop or two, embroidery, and so on, all stuck in without any idea of grouping or related sequence. Ah, I reflected, how different would be the scrap-book in the parlour of, say a German convent school. Anywhere along the Rhine would be found similar albums containing not very different scraps: the difference would be in the arrangement. The thing would be done on a plan. There would be an animal section, a section for holy pictures, a military section, a landscape section, and so on. While here in our glorious haphazard England the children are encouraged to allow their fancy free play. Whatever catches their eye they cut out and paste in: Bernard Shaw, a basket of kittens, the Little Flower, Kew Gardens . . . just lumped together anyhow. Splendid. The Reverend Mother still showed no signs of coming so I decided to go through the albums again and see whether I could not trace at least *some* sort of principle on which the scraps had been collected. Surely, I said to myself, the sister in charge of the class must sooner or later have betrayed her taste, if not her method, in what she allowed the little girls to bring along. "Now, children," I thought of her as saying. "Now, children, I want you all to look for something *gold* for our album. Go away now and see if by next lesson you can't find something nice and golden." (Or something sad, or square, or romantic, or Welsh, or whatever.) But as I turned the pages I could not find the key. There was absolutely nothing that predominated. Not even the size of the scraps was anything to go on. "So long as it fits," sister must have said. I decided, since Reverend Mother was evidently being fetched from a long way away, to go through the scraps a third time, applying a negative test this time, and see whether there was not something that had been left out which would give me the clue to the directing mind behind the collection. Sure enough, I was on the scent before I had got through the first volume. Eagerly I began on the second. "There isn't," I said as I turned the last page, "a single joke."

It is a common thing to find in the spiritual life souls who make rapid strides towards perfection, but whose development after a time seems to come to a standstill. They reach an impasse. So far and no farther: even sometimes a perceptible going back. We see this in others, and we are sometimes disturbingly aware of it in ourselves. Of course there may be a hundred other reasons for this but there is one which is not sufficiently pointed out, and that is a lack of integration in the soul's approach to God. Plenty of virtues are there, and plenty of practices, but the whole thing doesn't hang together; it is a patchwork and not a pattern; there is no synthesis. Why? Because very often there is something left out.

To many souls the call to some particular virtue—it may be poverty, external charity, penance, prayer—is so clear that the calls to other virtues are heard less clearly, and eventually are less listened to. The soul feels an obligation to that one aspect of God's service and mistakenly neglects the rest. This is to misconstrue utterly the action of grace. Attraction towards one good must imply a corresponding, though relative and proportionately lesser, attraction towards others. Obviously to go all out, for example in the practice of liturgical worship while neglecting the duties of a husband is to throw out the balance. If the inspiration to pursue evangelical poverty induces a hearty disgust for the rich, we have reason to suspect the genuineness of the inspiration. Indeed wherever there is exclusion, intolerance, bias, there is bound to be more of self than of spiritual motive. This is true of human relationships as well: if attraction towards one person induces revulsion from others, it is a sign that the affection is disordered. In the building of God's temple, the walls must rise evenly: there must be no impatient finishing of the façade while the parts less exposed to public admiration go unattended to. Such is human nature that even in spiritual things we get a craze for this and that, and our craze can well become a canker. The man who thinks that "there's only one thing that matters in the spiritual life" approaches God on too narrow a front. If a man believes that what God wants of him is active work for souls, he must practise more prayer, more penance; not less. If he feels that his vocation is towards solitude, he must be more careful, not less, about the claims upon his charity. And so on, right along the line. Even the virtues can become absorptive. They can swallow up other virtues altogether, and so upset the evenness of the whole. To be possessed by an ideal is all very well, but we must avoid being obsessed by it.

Serenity is the sheen of order, and the saints were serene because of the integrated lives they led. Not only was every energy in the same direction but every outward action tallied with the inward principle. All for God and nothing out of place. Why we get harassed is because not everything is for God, and because there are usually a few things out of place. Admittedly some of the saints who were raised up by God to stress certain virtues did so with a fire that draws our attention to one particular aspect of their sanctity while it dulls our perception of the rest, but this doesn't mean that they were one track. It is here, incidentally, that Western mysticism differs from mysticism in the East. The Buddhist conception of spirituality, and still more of asceticism, admits of exaggerations which would never be held up to admiration in the Christian world. The Church numbers some odd characters in her record, but she never boasts of fanaticism as being one of the marks of the true Faith. Indeed she seems to keep her oddities rather dark, smiling tolerantly, albeit rather uncertainly, at the goings on of some of the Fathers of the Desert. The limbs of the Mystical Body may be bruised and broken, but we must do our utmost to see that they are not distorted or deformed. The progress of the Christian saint is proportioned to the temperature of his love, and his love is expressed in every part of him. Christlike is the saint's approach, and in the life of Christ there were no false emphases, no overstatements. There is no denying that those who have followed Christ most closely have had their eccentricities and even their extravagances—it was the form their generosity took—but nobody would accuse them of aberrations or fixations. The nearest thing to a fixation in the mind of a saint is the preoccupation about loving God more. And if psychologists would classify this as an excess, it is an excess, a fixation, which we can well afford to suffer from.

Allowing then that the measured cultivation of the virtues —not one after another but all together, not one to the

neglect of the other but all together—is necessary to
supernatural progress, so also is the measured cultivation of
the sympathies. I mean that man can so often spoil the shape
of his sanctity by a certain thoughtless indifference which,
though not formulated at first, leads ultimately to hardness
and self-sufficiency. From being casual we can very easily
become callous. There must be no blind spots, nothing to
which our sympathies are closed. There are blind spots in
most of us. That is largely the trouble—we are, unless we
look carefully, blind to them. There is, as we have seen, a
design about our lives, and if we deviate from it ever so
slightly we are like jig-saw puzzles with some of the pieces
left out. Christ has redeemed the whole man, and man must
be given back to Him whole. There must be no missing bit.
What is our near-blind spot? What is our weakest suit? To
what do our sympathies not extend? Of what person, class,
habit of mind, trouble, outlook, suffering, problem, do we
find ourselves saying "I can't be bothered with that"? It
is of the first importance that we find out where our particular thoughtlessness lies, and that we face its implications.
It is then that we must substitute the missing sympathy.
Thoughtlessness is not the same as cruelty but it can often
have the same effect. As far as other people are concerned,
want of care and want of charity produce an almost equal
unhappiness. Our lack of sympathy—and sympathy is
entering into the mind of the other person, not merely
pitying him—can wither and blight at a time when an
effort to understand would bring infinite relief. Much of the
misery of life arises from not trying to see the other man's
point of view. "It's not my job." "I don't know the
people." "They are only children after all" (or "*only*
servants" or "*only* niggers"). "It's hardly my line." These
excuses can be betrayals. St. Peter's "I know not the man"
is hardly worse. We have no right to say that we know not

the man, woman, or child who is made after the image and likeness of God.

So much for the blind spots, but what about the open-eyed ones? We have dealt with the missing pieces which we have to look for, what about the missing pieces which we have hidden? If we have to admit to any of those, the progress of the puzzle is less satisfactory than ever. Obviously our lives are bound to lack cohesion if we cling to any one disrupting element. It may not even be a sin—though of course that would do it—but if it is the kind of reservation which we know to be clogging the intimate communion between the soul and God its influence will extend to every sphere of the soul's service, and for as long as it is consented to there will be no further progress. Such an obstacle would be, for instance, deliberately excluding any one person from our fullest charity, retaining an affection which is felt to be excessive but which we have not the courage to modify, keeping on with a line of study, or a hobby, or a recreation which is found to be a self indulgence, a distraction to our prayer and peace of mind, and something not in keeping with our vocation. While such malordered factors as these exist, the walls will never be complete. Not only will the gaps widen and admit influences which were never envisaged, but cracks will appear in other parts of the masonry.

Co-ordinated, then, must be our lives, not scattered and piecemeal according to whim, prejudice, and predilection: unsorted and eclectic they are by nature, harmonious only by grace. It is for us to be "compacted and fitly joined together," to use St. Paul's words to the Ephesians, "according to the operation in the measure of every part." (Or as the Westminster Version has it, "by means of every joint, part working in harmony with part".)

As I sat pondering these things in the cool silence of the convent parlour, the door opened and the Reverend

Mother came in. "I'm afraid I have kept you," she said, switching on the light for it was almost dark by this time, "but I see you've been looking at my scraps. I do them at night, you know, when I can't sleep. I find it soothes me. Isn't insomnia a dreadful thing, father?" "Dreadful," I said.

HEALTH

THE OBSERVATIONS that follow must be prefaced by this safeguard: they represent a purely private opinion and are not to be taken as a pronouncement from Rome on the subject. The Church, on the matter of health, is silent. So what is there to prevent one of its members becoming rather violent about health cranks? Anyway that is what I propose to do, and if any other member of the Church objects to it, let him.

As a principle we can lay down that all things being equal, health should never be the reason for not doing something worth while. In this respect it resembles money: money must never be the deciding cause. Risk it, I say, and see what happens. So far the general principle; now for the question of its application.

"But of course your health must come first." Must it? Certainly not if there is anything better to put before it. In the ordinary way the demands of health must be listened to—we go to bed if we have a high temperature or when there is danger of infecting others; we rest when we are exhausted; we eat what we believe to be good for us—but so often the ordinary way is found to be strewn with extraordinary conditions and situations. With the result that the necessities normally due to health become relative. Who would dare say that we owe more to our bodies than to the calls of charity? And yet we excuse ourselves without scruple on the plea that we aren't really well enough.

It is the melancholy experience of most people that there is no more effective screen than that of being a semi-invalid. If you are a complete invalid there's no difficulty whatever:

you are helpless, you can help nobody, the thing is simplicity itself. But if you are a near-crock you find yourself limping through life on the arms of others without ever having the least desire to be in your turn a crutch. The great thing to remember is that in the presence of some things—and this may be taken to mean most things—bodily well-being doesn't matter a bit.

"But I must keep fit for the sake of my work." This is a valid reason. But only up to a point. The greatest work is the work of charity. One's job is not one's religion. I should have thought it was better to risk being unfit for one's job in order to be certain of being fit for God. But I may be wrong. There are spiritual men who tell us that it is a delusion to imagine that God wishes to be placed above the work He gives us to do. In the general way perhaps it is. But it might not be. There are occasions when we are faced with two aspects of God's will: our duties conflict. All I am saying is that health is the first to be risked. The declared will of God is far more important than the hypothetical illness which clogs our activity.

There is another aspect of the work-health combination: risking one's health in order to do a particular work. This is again an occasion when I would say "Go ahead; risk it". Where in the former instance work is in danger of taking religion's place, in this connexion it occupies the position which nature—not to mention religion—means it to take. The body is adapted to labour, and who would not rather see an exhausted and even a sick body straining its last effort to perform a piece of work than know that something had been left unfinished because the worker was taking no chances with his health?

We have, as always, only to turn to the example of the saints to get a lead in this matter. Their approach was unmistakable. To them St. Paul's advice to the Romans about "spending no thought on nature and nature's appetites" covered the whole question of looking after oneself. Oh yes, granted they received special calls from God, granted their penances were helped out by extraordinary graces, granted they had been brought up tough and that everybody's standards were different in those days, etc. etc., there is no doubting the fact that almost without exception the saints were rash to the point of foolhardiness on the subject of their health. They horrified their friends, they exasperated their doctors, they allowed themselves some very funny ideas as to the virtue of prudence, but they did an enormous amount of work and became saints. Also, with the exception of St. Bernard, who admitted he had treated his body abominably, they never seem to have had any regrets. (One wonders whether St. Bernard was really sorry, and whether he would not have done exactly the same if he had had his life over again.) There are some things which would be so incongruous on the lips of the saints that the very sound of them should shame us into silence. "Not if it's raining, if you don't mind; you know how liable I am to chills." "But that would mean spending the night in the station." "I think another day in bed—just to be on the safe side." Yet we make these frightful remarks on the smallest provocation . . . when perhaps we are missing the chance of relieving another's mental suffering, when we might be bringing the light of the Gospel to someone who has been nerving himself for weeks to ask us about the Faith, when there is some work to be done which either won't be done at all if we don't do it or which will add considerably to the burdens of other people to perform.

One factor which weighs very much against us is the sloppy assistance which we receive whenever we put the question of our health to other people. Men who give us stimulating advice on almost any other line of conduct suddenly become grandmotherly and beg us for heaven's sake to wrap ourselves up in tissue paper. Friends who would not question our decision to spend the whole night playing bridge are shocked at the liberties we are taking with our health if we suggest getting up for an hour in the night to pray. There is apparently nothing dangerous to health in the hardships of the hunting field while there is every reason to fear an early death if one so much as fasts during Lent. The hair-shirt and the discipline are as nothing to the discomforts which men will put up with for the sake of pleasure. It is only when they put up with them for the sake of God that their friends begin to tremble for their health.

THE BENEFIT OF THE DOUBT

IT COMES as a shock to us sometimes to find how little we see into the minds of even those whom we think we know through and through. We imagine that we have reached a stage of intimacy where the other's reactions to a situation (or a person or a topic or anything else) can be estimated with certainty—foreseen in fact—and then suddenly we come up against the unexpected, the unpredicted, and we have to admit that our knowledge had its limitations after all. It is not only when we are let down that this happens—I am not thinking now of the gloomy occasions when we come away disappointed in someone whom we have trusted and looked up to—it happens over the most absurd things. Always it leaves us with the hollow feeling of insufficiency: we realize with brutal clarity that in this world there really *is* nothing that is satisfying. It is not that we blame the other person for not coming up to our expectations but that we despair of ever being able to reach a full mutual understanding in any human relationship. This illuminating remark of his (or this equally significant silence) does not mean that a friendship has come to an end, it is just that I know we were miles away from one another when I thought there was absolute identity of mind. If I blame anyone it is myself—for having laid myself open to such avoidable disillusion.

Disraeli says somewhere that mutual love produces a true intuitive sense in people whereby they know at once what is going on in each other's minds. It doesn't. It can't do. The statement was made lightly. What Disraeli probably meant was that the bond of sympathy between two people could be so close that things like secrets, reserves, suspicions and so on could be ruled out. The sharing of thoughts belongs to telepathy, not to love. Besides (this is put forward tentatively, and it doesn't really matter anyway) doesn't understanding come first, forming the basis of love, rather than as one of the effects? Understanding is often taken for granted in the impatience of love, but surely it isn't something superadded once the affections have got under way, coming as a sort of guarantee? You can't really love what you don't at all understand. Whereas you can understand what you don't at all love. Which suggests that you must get sympathy and agreement before you can get anything else. In the full flowering of love there is obviously both, and the mutual understanding becomes more wide and more penetrating according to the quality of the love. All I am saying here is that love does not strictly *supply* understanding, it supposes it.

In this life there is bound to be a point beyond which our human understanding cannot go. God alone comprehends His creatures. He knows what is in man, we don't. We can only guess. This is not surprising since, apart from the fact that we have only finite minds, we have first of all only limited data to go upon in our effort to follow the workings of another's mind, and in the second place there are natural barriers which would be enough to make full understanding impossible.

As regards the limited data, all that is provided are external things: effects. It is only through a man's work—what he says and does—that we can get at his mind. He can tell us what his thoughts are, but even then we have only his word for it—his external word. The outward is a true enough index of the inward as far as it goes, but it doesn't take us very far. Steam doesn't give us the nature of boiling water. This habit of judging—of *having* to judge if we judge at all—by the evidence of the senses leads us even to the belief that we can know people whom we have never so much as spoken to. This is merely an exaggeration of the same principle: that we never meet the man save in his work. "I know from his paintings exactly what sort of a man he is; in fact I feel I know the man himself." "This writer touches something in me which gives me the key to the whole of his character." "The part he takes upon the stage isn't really a part; it's him, and it's as if I knew him as a friend." This sort of remark, made about complete strangers, has an element of truth about it. We do in a way know the man—we can form a fair estimate about what sort of scenes and good looks he admires, what sort of jokes he enjoys, what sort of principles he professes—but it is in such an inadequate way that it can hardly be called knowledge at all. We would know more if we read about him; which is not the way we get to know our friends.

Then there is the other limiting factor: the barriers which nature puts up and so prevents the fullest harmony of intercourse. Though sharing a common ancestor we differ from one another so much that perfect agreement in all things is not even a dream. It couldn't be. (And incidentally, among fallen mankind, it wouldn't work.) Not only are we so separated from each other by temperament that even in a family there is often complete lack of understanding, but in other ways as well there are great gulfs fixed by nature which the best will in the world can never wholly bridge. Can I ever really enter into the mind of a person of a different nationality? Can I feel about things the same as a person who is years older or younger than myself—or am I learning to feel the same if I am younger, and remembering my feelings if I am older? What about the difference of sex—do men and women ever really think alike? And class—can social grading be written off

altogether? In all these things it is not a question of sympathy.
Of course we can have sympathy, and I am coming to that
in a minute. It is a question as to whether our understanding of another's nature can penetrate so deeply as to
deserve the name of knowledge. And we conclude that
strictly speaking it can't.

Since the problem of life is to a large extent the problem of
human intercourse, we had better get all this right. Though
these barriers which we have been considering exist by
nature, there is no reason why they should not be got over
by faith. Allowing that faith and charity do not give us
infallible insight into our neighbour's brain, there is no
reason why they should not be used to get over his natural
obstacles. Naturally we are *other* from our neighbour,
supernaturally we are one with him. Class, age, race, and
the rest can be treated as if they didn't exist.

Thus we get back to Disraeli's assertion, giving to his
word "love" the specific direction of charity. And if our
charity is the outcome of our understanding, it is of the
first importance that we learn to understand. Oddly enough
we know that we have to try and love our neighbour; what
we forget is that we have to try and understand him. "I
can't understand that man." "It's a mentality I can't
understand." Have you ever for a moment tried to?
Solomon was never wiser than when he asked God to give
him "an understanding heart" with which to rule his people.
If our prayer of petition took this form morning and
evening we would both please God and stand a better chance
of pleasing our neighbour. Not only do we evade the
obligation of entering into the minds of others but we
sometimes take care that others should not enter into ours.
Too ready to look for sympathy from our friends, we do
exactly the opposite with regard to those who we fear
might become bores if they came any closer. Beyond the

natural barriers we put up a ring of built-up defences—
aloofness and inaccessibility—which are calculated to daunt
the most adventuresome of bores. But how do we know
that we are not repelling a soul in need of a sympathy or
a solution which we alone are intended by God to provide?
And perhaps that other person, that potential nuisance, is
in his turn an angel in disguise sent by God on an errand
of mercy to us. There are few more winning virtues than
that of understanding. "I found I could talk to him at once."
One feels about the saints that they radiated happiness by
going out to others and so inviting a return. The bond of
understanding was immediate. There was no calculation.
"Is it worth it?" "He may turn out to be frightful." "I
don't see why I should take the first step." This sort of thing
never entered the heads of the saints; or if it did it was dis-
missed at once.

   To be ready to give oneself out to others means that one
has to take risks, and one has to believe in human nature.
One takes the risk of being snubbed, misunderstood and
ridiculed. This is all in order: it is in the best tradition. As
to one's confidence in human nature it must be infinite.
It is the only way. If we don't think people are generous
enough to respond, they won't respond. If we believe in
them, show them that we think them capable of the heights,
they will. A man will go one better than his best in order to
live up to what an idealist believes of him. Father Bede
Jarrett's extraordinary influence over young men was simply
due to this: they hadn't the heart to disillusion him—that
was the first step—and then they found, to their surprise
very often, that they were capable of being what he expected
them to be. Give a man credit for the good that is in him and
the good will multiply under your hand like the loaves and
fishes in the hands of the disciples. If you doubt him, then
swallow your doubt—give him the benefit of it. What

has all this to do with understanding? It has this to do with
it: understanding is that part of faith which fishes about in
another man's soul for the noble things that are there but
which might otherwise never see the light of day. Faith in
human nature to produce the best: the same faith in every
member of it. No amount of disappointments must ever
destroy that.

If I look for the best in others I must give out the best
that is in myself. Goodness is magnetic—just as understanding is magnetic. Not that my goodness is switched on
to meet an occasion—any more than my interest in bringing
out the goodness in others is self-conscious and tiresome—
but it is something to be cultivated and directed. It is our
Lord's "for them do I sanctify myself": not now merely for
my own benefit but for the benefit of the world at large.
For the world at large, moreover, and not simply for the
world at home. There are some who possess the greatest
natural and supernatural gifts, but who restrict their
influence to an immediate few. I have come across only one
sad deathbed in my life and that was of a man who felt that he
had wasted his talent by narrowing the field of his aposto-
late. He had lived and worked only for those who had
interested him. "And if I had lived for every one," he told
me, "I would have found them all interesting." As it was,
the world for him had been divided into the bores and the
non-bores, the bores being vastly in the majority. To the
saint there are no real bores, because he digs so deep that
what is worth while is eventually discovered, however
deeply hidden.

A person is remembered for the influence he has had upon
others much more than for the position he has risen to in his
career, and the power of influencing others is more dangerous
to neglect than to use. The man who wears his heart upon
his sleeve is to be preferred to the man who leaves it in a

drawer, and though it is only too possible for would-be apostles to turn the spotlight upon themselves instead of upon God in their dealings with souls, it would be a mistaken policy to assume that the only safety lay in a darkened stage.

To conclude, and to get back to where we started. We can't hope to know others as we should like to, but we should make it our business to know them as well as we can. Which can take us pretty far. In our knowledge of God, faith takes us pretty far. And God is far more *other* from us than our neighbour is. We know God: we know our neighbour. We know not merely *about* God; we know *Him*. We know not merely about our neighbour; we know him. Up to a point in each case. But truly nevertheless. Inadequate knowledge but true. "This is eternal life, that you know God and Jesus Christ whom He hath sent." Just as we know God from His outward utterance, His works, so we know our fellow human beings from their outward utterance, their works . . . our knowledge deepening according to our generosity or sympathy of approach. We have quoted the saints as being masters of human intercourse, but if we want a text-book we can go one better than the *Lives of the Saints* and pick up the Gospel. In the Model Man, Christ, we have the solution to the whole problem of human relationship: yielding Himself for others and inviting—continuing to invite because He will not allow His confidence in mankind to be beaten down—at the same time a return. "And I if I be lifted up will draw all things unto myself." *Draw* all things: the magnetic force of love—as shown in sacrifice.

TRUE AND FALSE REST

It is in the nature of man to seek for rest. Not that he is lazy but simply that rest is next in the sequence of being: it is the end (literally) of activity. Spiritual people look for rest in God, material people look for rest in creatures. Then there is a third lot of people who can neither be called spiritual nor material, and who look for rest in vacancy. These are they who for one reason or another—sometimes for quite lofty reasons and sometimes for no formulated reasons at all but because they are made that way—strip themselves of preferences, interests, satisfactions, both emotional and physical, and so, for a time, find rest. This is the approach of the Buddhist and Stoic philosopher resulting in the ἀπάθεια of the ancients. This rest is negative, and, by Gospel standards, all wrong. Allowing that we are not of set purpose among those who are stuffing themselves up to the lid of their capacity with carnal delights, and are seeking to find temporary rest that way, it is as well that we avoid the mistake of looking for rest in emptiness. A peace that is negative and sterile is no true peace. Such is not the peace, at any rate, which Christ came to bring upon the earth. "Not as the world giveth, do I give unto you," and though nature can procure for us a semblance of peace—even a quite legitimate and non-guilty peace—it is not the peace in God which we are discussing here.

The point of this essay is to explain the terms used by the mystics when writing about rest: a false application is quite enough to put people off reading such invaluable authors as St. John of the Cross, Ruysbroeck, and Dionysius the Areopagite. We are told for instance that the soul must rest in its restlessness, that not only is bodily rest to be written off as unattainable in any degree of security in this life but that rest in outward standards and forms is not to be hoped for either; that though God alone is to be rested in, it is not for the rest He affords that we must search for Him; and that even when we have found our way to Him and are treading it with the confidence born of faith, we must not, so long as we are still in this life, expect to *feel* the sense of rest. All this is puzzling and perhaps a little putting off.

Anyway it is clear that the love which is selfish desires a quite different sort of rest from the love which is unselfish. The greater the love, the greater the longing to rest in the object of it. The hunger and thirst after justice, the craving for God, the passionate desire (which is far more common than people think) to be dissolved and to be with Christ, begets a rest which is truly rest, but which is so far from being passive that it produces the dynamic activities of the saints. It is rest in the sense that all the faculties of such a soul are, because they are in the same direction, at rest: there is no disharmony in their operation. But there is certainly no lack of operation. On this showing the rest is not, obviously, restful. So little is it perceived in the senses, so little does it minister to outward peace, that though enjoyed deep down in the soul it is seldom felt to be much of a solace. The other kind of rest—whether it is the satisfaction resulting from the undisturbed and undisputed enjoyment of creatures or the calm arising from the elimination of trouble—is felt, while it is going on, to be much more of a solace. But then those who enjoy it can never depend upon its going on. Obviously if you place your peace and happiness in the comfort of a well-served meal, a fire, and an amusing book, you have, on the occasion when this happy combination is achieved, peace. If your approach is along the other avenue and you have managed to quell the causes of ordinary distress such as interruption, noise, anxiety, pain, inordinate desire, worry and so on, you do certainly possess, for as long as the smooth surface of your ordered calm is not lashed up by accident or malice, happiness. But what is the good of either of these rests—if the whole time you are enjoying it you know at the back of your mind that something may come along and take it away? The rust and the moth consume, robbers break through and steal: the only safe place for a first class treasure is in heaven.

"But may I never rest in creatures?" you may ask. "Are there no human satisfactions which can be leant on? Leaving aside the well-served meal and so on, aren't there pleasures of the intellect, spiritual pleasures, pleasures to do with science, art, nature, study, work for other people in which a man may safely place his rest?" All these things may be enjoyed for what they are worth, would be the answer, but they may not be fully rested in. They must be held in a loose hand. They are valuables only in so far as they are seen to have been lent to us: as soon as we appropriate them and look upon them as our own we are misusing them. Indeed as soon as we stretch out our hand to possess them they show their insufficiency by letting us down: our very greed tells us we shall never be satisfied: we shall want more and more and more. The treasure, however, that is buried in heaven holds out a different promise: our craving, though never granted satisfaction in this life, is never subject to dissatisfaction. The love of God, which knows where to place its rest, may be restless in its craving but it is not greedy for its gratification: it puts up with its hunger because in faith it is at rest.

"If it's as complicated as that," you may say, "the other

solution *does* appear to be the only one: flight from creatures is the only guarantee that they won't be wrongly rested in." Flight is one way, but it is the way of solving a problem by burying it. Creatures and talents may not be buried. Problems may not be buried. The problem of resting in creatures or flying from them can be met only by doing what our Lord and the saints did with it—which is by doing neither. God's creatures may be, indeed must be, loved. Provided there is no conflict between the love we have of them and the love we have of God, creatures are so many helps towards God. God Himself surveyed the work of His hands and saw that it was good. But though it is good, we can be bad about it. We can love it wrongly. We can so love it, rest in it, as to exclude the love of the Creator that made it. But this does not mean that we have to uproot the good for fear of turning it into a bad; it means that we have to correct the bad in us which refuses to see the good of God's creation as God sees it. The fall of man has set a chasm between God's earthly and God's heavenly creation, and though Christ Himself has come to bridge the gulf it is all too often our mistake and sometimes sinful folly that we create divisions of our own.

MORE ABOUT REST

THE CRAVINGS and the heartsearchings of the mystics are sometimes envied by us who find it's all we can do to scrape together a presentable desire for the things of the spirit. We think of these favoured souls as swooning in a continuous state of devotion, as languishing from the very violence of their joy, as being transported into realms of pleasure more rare and exquisite than anything that can be imagined by the unenlightened mind of man. What we forget is that the true lover of God is the one who sees how worthy God is of love and how little he, the lover, is giving to Him. In thinking he has no love, the mystic in fact has no rest. No rest that he can call rest. But rest which, in the foregoing essay, we have defined as rest. No rest in the feelings but rest in the unity of his desire. Just as someone judging the state of the mystic from without would never dream of saying that the soul was without love, so in the same way it would be wrong to say that the soul was without rest. It is rather that the true lover of God has no *feelings* either of love or of rest.

They rest truly, whether they feel it or not, who possess themselves in unity, simplicity, and truth. Such souls are prepared to go restless, and this is true rest because it means that nothing now can disturb their essential peace. Their very upsets are taken as the will of God, their balance is— as far as it can be in this life—assured. All other rest is subject to interruption. Let the philosopher who goes about his business without the knowledge of God or the help of grace subdue the three disturbances of activity, imagery, and desire, he still has nothing but a barren and

96

flattened peace. It is so much static water. What he wants is the peace which surpasses understanding, the peace of Christ. Where peace rests upon a surface it is bound to fall through.

This question of what are the only foundations of true security shows up the difference between the real and the bogus mystic at once. And there are some souls who, though by no means to be classed among imposters, are yet inclined to follow the bogus in that they account their recollection as being more important than their love. The quietist, who is certainly a bogus mystic, is so anxious not to be troubled by any sort of act that he sits still in a luxurious void. The saint, on the other hand, lives in no such walled-up vacuum: he radiates his ardent energy outwards towards man and upwards towards God. Yet he has true rest, and the other hasn't. Longing is the expression of true rest, suppression of longing is the expression of false. The quietist dares not think of our Lord in his prayer, or try and unite himself with Him, in case his mind fills up with thoughts: he wants it to be empty so that there can be complete abstraction. The saint has no such fears: he makes it his aim to unite himself as closely as he possibly can with Christ, both in his prayer and out of it, whether his mind fills up with thoughts or not. For him it is a question of keeping away interfering thoughts, not loving ones. He will find as a fact that his thoughts will tend to become fewer and less distinct, but this is not strictly in his control. His one idea is to unite himself with God in prayer and with God's will out of it. The soul that avoids union with the will of God, whether in prayer or out of it, for fear of disturbing its peace of mind is putting itself in the absurd position of saying that freedom from disturbance is more important than that which freedom from disturbance is intended to promote. "Oh no, Father, I could never go to

Lourdes; much too distracting." It is people like that who will find it distracting in heaven.

Thus it looks in the last analysis as if the soul which serves God in spirit and in truth enjoys a very unusual kind of peace: not the satisfying inward rest which we would have expected nor the outward rest of having everything in order and nothing left out, but a rest which consists in contentment at having sacrificed both to the will of God. There is no peace for the wicked—this we can understand—but it seems a little hard that there should be none for the good, either. But that is the way of it, and they, if any, can take the rough with the smooth. They are serene.

POSSESSIVENESS

IN THE relationship between friends there is bound to be an element of possessiveness. It is only as well that we should be able to claim a right kind of possessiveness and not merely have to admit to the wrong kind. If we are greedy for the other's affection, demanding a monopoly and constant attention, then of course we shall try and run our friend. The manager-companion is an abomination, and his spirit spells death to the easy disinterestedness which must never be lost sight of in a friendship. Partners are never on entirely the same footing, but if one of the two vests himself with an authority which is at all masterful the balance can hardly be maintained. Nevertheless, though ownership may be something wrong among friends it is only the exaggeration of something right. We naturally want to improve the people we are fond of, and the more fond of them we are the more this desire comes up. We want to make them into what we believe them capable of being. To want to alter our friends is simply the effect of our idealistic conception of them. An affection which exhibits not the least wish to influence the other person is either entirely blind, or else too indifferent to deserve the name of love. The trouble is usually the reverse: we want to alter the other person too much, to fashion him after our own image and likeness. We want to see our handiwork revealed in the character of a fellow human being. We want to have a living memorial to ourselves. Possessiveness can spoil everything—not only the quality of the relationship but also the plan of God.

The practical question is how to tell when we are being possessive in the right way and when in the wrong way. We can start off with the most altruistic sentiments in the world, wishing to guide another along the paths of high virtue for his own sake and for his own sake alone, and then we find ourselves gradually tailing off until we are moved by a selfishness which questions, criticises, resents the least deviation from principles which we have insisted upon as conditioning our friendship. Obviously in something as unique as the relationship between two human beings there can be no generalizations; there are, however, indications which show the drift. Let us examine some.

If, rather than pointing out the way to my friend, I am bent upon driving him, then there is clearly something too absorptive about my affection. The thing will end in a whine of nagging, reproach, and self-justification. If I take offence when my advice is turned down, it means that I am ordering my friend about, and not merely offering my help for what it is worth. You may say that we are there to give counsel to our friends. And so we are. But not to insist upon its being taken. Where there is no freedom there is no true friendship, and to some natures there is nothing so offending as the use of this liberty in others. Large natures are never offended in this way, though large natures may very well be hurt. When we are offended it is our vanity that suffers, when we are hurt it is ourselves.

Again, if I make a monopoly of the other's affection —or if I seriously yield the monopoly of mine—the door is thrown open to friendship's greatest menace, jealousy. Jealousy cramps, shrivels, withers. Charity expands. All too human is the love which excludes; gloriously Christian is the charity which embraces in its sweep all that come by the way. Because we are more fond of X than of any one else, we need not be dismissive to Y and Z. If our love is founded on the right thing our affection for X will make us care more, not less, for Y and Z and every one else in the alphabet. Such certainly is the love of Christ for us, and in the all important matter of love we should aim at nothing less than possessing a Christlike attitude of heart. At any rate I for one dare boast that I shall not be happy until I feel towards all that warmth which I bear towards those whom I count my closest friends. "The means to gain happiness in life," writes Tolstoy in his diary, "is to throw out from oneself in all directions like a spider an adhesive web of love, and to catch in it all that comes: an old woman, a child, a girl, a policeman." Such a charity is more than merely the means of gaining human happiness—or at all events can be made to mean more.

As a pendant to what has been said about the monopoly of another's affection, a paragraph might be added about the monopoly of another's time. If we resent interruption, if we regard as wasted the hours not spent together, if we are exacting about future plans or querulous about broken appointments, if we expect an account of what has been going on in our absence, then we are trading unduly upon our privilege. The whole thing would simplify itself if we could look upon ourselves as existing for the benefit of the other person instead of imagining that our friendship has been given for what *I* on *my* side can get out of it. We serve Christ in our friend, and in the service of Christ there must be no grudging of time or energy or trust. Does this lay us open to endless hurt? Of course it does, but after all why not? It is right that our loves should cost us more than our hates. We suffer doubts about our friend only that we may make acts of confidence about him. His apparent neglect gives us the willies, his weaknesses drive us into paroxysms of anxiety, the possibility of his getting bored with us keeps us awake for weeks *but all this is the stuff of friendship.* We must not fear our fears, or even fight them. We must laugh at them. They have no substance. They are merely the willies. They arise from the desire to own the thing we love, to master, to transform. And ownership must be left to God. Provided we retain the power to take our possessiveness lightly we shall never be guilty of exercising undue control.

CONTEMPLATION

To the average layman the idea of contemplation is both unpractical and putting off. "Not for us." Granted that the contemplative life cannot be fitted into the normal layman's programme, there is nothing to prevent contemplative prayer finding a place in it. St. Augustine defines contemplation as "the directing of a serene and straight look on the object to be regarded . . . the striving to understand those things that really and supremely are". If this is all it is—and St. Augustine ought to know—then it is the appropriate act of religion. All are bound to the virtue of religion, and it would seem therefore that it must be everybody's vocation to direct a straight look at God when setting out to pray. Certainly it is everybody's vocation to try to understand those things that really and supremely are. It looks horribly as if we are all called to be contemplatives.

Notice one thing about the above quotation: it speaks of striving to understand. Striving, not succeeding. In the same way the soul is described as directing its gaze, not enjoying its vision. True, in the act of perfect contemplation the faculties of the soul are at rest in their proper object, God, but contemplative prayer can begin long before there is any appreciable rest. Unfortunately St. Augustine's definition is not complete. As it stands it almost suggests that all you have to do to become a contemplative is to focus the eye of your soul, try to understand truth, and there you are. This would be all right if contemplation were within the scope of man's unaided endeavour. But it

isn't. Man can train himself up to a point when it is exceed-
ingly likely that he will receive the gift of contemplation,
but beyond this he cannot go. Contemplation is a gift from
God. We may all be called to receive the gift from God, but
the whole point of a gift is that it is freely given. It can be
led up to but not strictly deserved or merited. St. Augustine
is evidently concerned with the early stages—the disposing
of the soul. He would have been the first to admit with St.
John of the Cross that the act of contemplation was one
of receiving rather than one of giving. It is as if the soul
were expected to give until it had no more to offer; an
impasse follows; then comes God to give in His turn and in
a new currency—leaving Himself free henceforward to
give or take according to His pleasure.

But to get back to St. Augustine's definition, observe
that he wants the look towards God to be straight and
serene. If this means anything it means that we must not
bend back our gaze upon ourselves. And that we must
not fuss. A straight look is one that does not analyse, does
not flinch, does not shift from side to side. We must be
occupied with God in our prayer and not with the thought
of how we are praying. A serene look is one which is
indifferent to the visibility. In praying we must be un-
ambitious about our prayer. The particular state or level
we have reached is a matter of no consequence. This must
be left to God. The disposition most necessary to contemplation is receptivity, and if the soul is busy about its
reactions it can hardly be smooth enough to react. Take
the case of Our Lady: all her life she had been receptive
to the least movement of grace, and when the Angel came
with his message there was nothing in the way. Her gaze
was direct and unclouded by selfish interest. If she had
worried about exactly how direct and unclouded it was her
response would necessarily have been less immediate. Can

we think of Mary wondering, as she travelled to visit her
cousin, whether she was loving her unborn Child correctly?
Can we imagine her worrying, as she knelt before Him at
Bethlehem or stood below Him at the foot of the cross,
whether she was not perhaps sacrificing the prayer of quiet
to a prayer more directly connected with the senses?
Straight and serene was her prayer if anyone's was . . . the
kind of prayer that treasured for her in her heart those
things that really and supremely are.

But surely, it may be objected, there are times when
it is quite impossible for us to keep a steady gaze fixed in
the right direction? What about those occasions when
suffering, or disappointment, or anxiety, or a cold in the
head, or an undeserved rebuke, or what not, knocks us
quite off our balance, and when our prayer is simply an
undefined ramble without form or frame or recognizable
direction? Even so (would be the answer) in *intention* the
prayer is serene and straight. It is like a man wandering up
a mountain: he sees straight to the summit but his feet
tread a winding path that gets lost in the thicket and behind
the rock. We, when our preoccupations become too much
for us, can still *direct* our operations towards God. For a
time we shall miss the sense of smoothness on the surface
of the soul, for a time we shall wonder whether there *is*
an object towards which our efforts turn. But it is only a
surface smoothness that suffers; the depths can be kept calm
enough. It is only a mental wondering; there is no specula-
tion in the soul. While as to those things that really and
supremely are, we are ready enough to forgo the understanding of them in this life provided always that we hope
to understand them in the next.

THE PRAYER OF PETITION

IT IS very easy to become snobbish in prayer and look down upon asking God for things. St. Thomas gives the lie to this attitude of mind when he defines prayer as "an activity of the practical intellect chiefly consisting in petition". He is not talking here of contemplation, nor is there any discussion as to what is the highest form that prayer can take. He is merely saying that when you get down to it prayer is asking. And when you think of it—as when you think of most of St. Thomas's startling statements—it must be. Prayer is the human mind looking for something in the direction where it knows that something to be. Even if the soul is only exposing its miseries there is the implied cry for help. And this is asking. If it is expressing sorrow for sin there is the implied cry for pardon. Gratitude and praise are perhaps the most selfless forms of prayer, but even here we are asking God to listen.

Another form of snobbishness in prayer is shown in the idea that when asking for things we are necessarily displaying too much activity for the requirements of pure prayer. This is of course sheer rubbish. For one thing the activity of suffering, or delighting, or sneezing, doesn't interfere with pure prayer, so why should praying? For another thing, except in the case of certain supernatural states of prayer, activity of some sort is essential. Read again the definition of St. Thomas quoted above. The same saint, in another place, calls prayer "an activity of the virtue of religion". It is bustle, not activity, that militates against the serenity required for interior prayer, and then only the kind of bustle that is admitted in the will. If all operation were to cease there would be no response to the action of grace, there would be no expression of the virtue of religion. The very word "ex-pression" connotes a going out, a pro-pulsion towards something.

Not only is prayer an activity of religion but it is, because it regards God directly, the best act. It is higher than the act of charity towards one's neighbour because it is the expression of one's charity towards God. Consequently any act performed prayerfully—whether related to one of the virtues or not—*becomes* an act of virtue. Re-creations, undertakings, human relationships—not to mention the more obvious things like sufferings, misunderstandings, loneliness and doubt—acquire a sacred character under the cover of prayer. Caussade's illuminating phrase "the sacrament of the present moment" means precisely this. The human will directed towards God, recognizing its dependence upon God, intent upon performing all that the perfect service of God involves . . . this, although it be wordless, is the attitude of mind which we associate with perfect prayer. And who would say that petition was not compatible with such a disposition?

Unless the place of petition is allowed and even assured in all but the purely passive and extraordinary prayers there is the danger of divorcing prayer from life. The mistake is common enough of thinking that prayer is a thing apart, a sanctifying exercise to be tacked on to everyday existence but in no way related to the course and character of every happening. The function of prayer is not primarily to help in the ordering of our lives. Its primary function is to give glory to God. But the more it is part of our lives the better.

There is this also to be considered, that where other activities of religion may express one or other of its virtues. prayer—in its most generous form at any rate—expresses them all. To service, to justice, to penance there is in prayer the added and all blessed quality of love. Who ever heard of a love that was too proud to ask?

The saints? Did they ask for things from God? Certainly they did, that is why people asked them for their prayers. That is why we ask them now to pray whenever we want anything. Ah, you will say, but that is different: they may have asked on behalf of others but surely it is unworthy to think of them as asking for what they themselves wanted. Not at all. They asked for what they wanted most, but then what they wanted most was not what we want most: they asked for God's will. They hungered for more and more and more of God. And what is more, they got what they wanted. Following their lead and the Gospel injunction we can, in our prayer, do worse than "seek first the Kingdom of God", and we shall find that all these things which we ask for shall be added to us. All these things? Why not, if they are things which are to our soul's health?

"Ask of the gods," says Socrates, "only for good things." This is sound enough as far as it goes. Christ goes farther than Socrates. "Ask for anything in my name," says Christ, "and it shall be given to you." Anything. But particularly for the Father's will. Anyway *ask*.

ON BEING BOGUS

THE PURPOSE of this essay is not to give the signs of
false mysticism but merely to warn would-be mystics that
there is a sort of sham spirituality to which even the best
intentioned are very often liable. It doesn't matter much
if we try and strike attitudes before other people because
sooner or later someone—a wise director perhaps, or an
exasperated friend—will tell us not to be idiotic, but it
does matter a good deal if we try and strike attitudes before
God or before ourselves, because it is quite likely that God
won't tell us and it is absolutely certain that we won't tell
ourselves.

It is not that we set out to deceive, or that at any time
we yield to the temptation of hypocrisy. (We can do this
of course at any time, but I am not thinking here of the
conscious humbug.) It is more that we form a false estimate
of the demands of the spiritual life, and base our conduct
upon a collection of half truths. We see the need for
sacrifice, but we miss its character. We grasp the idea of
love, but we apply it wrongly. We follow in the wake of
the saints, but noisily—with the emphasis on the less
significant things. Spiritual books can be a menace to some
people, and the most carefully worded sermon can be
misunderstood. The soul that would embark upon the
interior life must avoid the snare of saying: "This is the
way for me, and I am going to stick to it all my life whatever anyone says." It sounds an admirable thing to resolve
but he must not do it. We may not thus cramp the action
of grace, we may not dictate to the Holy Ghost. How dare
we know what way is best for us? How dare *we* choose the

mould to which we must yield? The whole point of
yielding to a mould is that we yield. Once we start choosing,
we cease to yield.

If we ask ourselves frankly what it is about a certain
saint that appeals to us, about a certain type of spirituality,
about a certain mode of behaviour, we are often forced to
admit that behind a lot of excellent reasons lurks our old
friend glamour. Mortification is seen in terms of hair-
shirts. Prayer is measured by the clock. Saints are divided
according to whether they are my kind or not my kind.
The bar to which all questions are brought for decision is
not the mind of Christ but the fashion of thought induced
by some authority who may be all very well in helping
other people but who may not be intended by God for
us. Loyalty to an author, and even to a saint, may be
entirely misplaced. The saint was a saint because he found
what was God's way for him and stuck to it. It is not for
me to rediscover that way: I have to find out what is God's
way for me. It may or may not be the way of my saint—let's
hope it is, for it will make it easier having his example and
help—but the thing to remember is that detachment from
conceptions is as important in the spiritual life as detachment from creatures. Perhaps more so, since not only do
circumstances very often rid us of our possessions while they
very seldom rid us of our ideas, but it is also much more
difficult to change habits of mind than habits of body.

If there is one axiom more than another which we would
do well to get right at the outset it is that God rewards
only His own works. If we try to put across any other
works we may get rewarded with lavish generosity by our
friends or by any one else whom we are eager to impress,
but we shall receive no sort of approval from God. In the
sight of God works are not judged objectively. He does
not say: "More and bigger works, please. You are not

giving Me the heroics that are being performed by the man next door, so of course you cannot expect his rewards." What God says is: "Don't worry about the man next door except to wonder at his generosity. What you have to do is to go straight on with the work which I have given *you*. Works aren't measured one against another, and if I find you picking out stunt works which are outside My scheme for your perfection I shall not be pleased. People who busy themselves with making towers to the sky are apt to hear such a babel of voices that they miss the still small voice of My inspiration. The towers that are to be built must rest on very sure foundations indeed, they must be planned and contracted by Me."

The Gospel tells us not to be wolves in sheep's pelts. Wolves are not condemned; it is the masquerade that is condemned. It would be just as wrong for sheep to appear in the guise of wolves. If I am a wolf I thank God for it: if I am a sheep I thank God just the same. What I would like to have been is not of the slightest consequence. The moment I start dressing up so as to play the part of another, however holy, I am being false to myself and false to God. Truth is not only avoiding lies, it is conformity. "Live according to what you are and you will grow." To grow in one direction when we should be growing in another is an altogether bogus growth. To live according to what we are not, when we should be living according to what we are, is an altogether bogus life. Growth: life: truth. Look after the truth: the life and growth will follow.

SHEPHERD AND SHEEP

WE TAKE it for granted that the Good Shepherd goes out of His way to find His sheep, but we forget that it is in the power of the sheep to go out of their way to find their Shepherd. Gregarious we are by nature, but charitable—both towards the Shepherd and the other members in the flock—by grace. Now if souls are different from one another, then the operation of grace differs in each particular case. Here there can be no generalizations, no slogans, no panaceas. Not only does Christ invite each soul, one by one, along a way of its own, but the particular attraction which He exercises is differently felt in each individual. It seems that He appeals according to His individuality, and we respond according to ours. Obviously there can be nothing stereotyped or inevitable about such a relationship. Every new relationship is unique, a wonder such as nobody has ever experienced before. It is in a special way that each sheep must get to know his Shepherd; not in the way of the rest of the herd.

This means that each sheep, however loyally it follows the flock, must maintain its own personality. It would be a mistake for us to select a saint and model ourselves upon him. The saints became saints in their way—which was God's way for them. We must become saints in ours—which is God's way for us. The way for every one is of course the way of Christ: we model ourselves on Him. But this does not mean that in the strict sense we *imitate* Him—this could be done by playing a part—it means that we so arrange our lives as to relive His life in ours. From trying to see things as He sees them, love people as He loves them,

suffer the upsets of life in union with His Passion, we come
to that reproduction and sharing of life which is the Way
and the Truth and the Life. It is then that all our actions
are done "in Christ": it is the "putting on of Christ" which
is urged by St. Paul. But notice that they are still *our* actions,
it is still the putting on of Christ upon *ourselves*. Else
would we be no longer free; else would we no longer have
the greatest of His gifts to give back again to Him.

If we are to develop our own line we must not forget that
our fellow sheep are equally expected to develop theirs. In
following Christ along their way they will cut across the
line by which we are trying to follow Him in ours. This is
where the trouble begins. It is this that explains the occasions
where we find good people at variance with one another.
Within the same shelter there will be devout sheep misunderstanding, suspecting, resenting the ways of other sheep.
Disagreement is perhaps inevitable; it is discord that must
be avoided. The sheep will have to put up with the suffering of not being able to square another's practice with
theory, but they must prevent themselves from tearing
the wool off each other's backs. In fact there must be such a
harmony resulting from the related lives within the fold
that others from outside may be attracted to follow the
same leadership. Our Lord Himself says so: "Others there
are who are not of this flock . . . they also must come."
And for each who comes, He has a different welcome, a
different affection.

Thus as far as we are concerned the condition of our
getting to know the Good Shepherd is simply being true
to ourselves and to Him—in other words being sincere. We
must not, like Jacob, disguise ourselves in order to obtain
our blessings. On the contrary we must, as David did when
he turned down the offer of Saul's armour, go into battle
with the equipment which suits *us*. We must wear what God

wants us to wear, even if we rather fancy ourselves in something more spectacular. There must be no sham, no make-
up. Our friends may have quite other ideas as to what suits
us, we may have quite other pictures of ourselves, but the
only thing that matters is the idea which exists of us in the
mind of God. Find that out, make for it, and we shall be
holy—and happy as well.

Because sheep differeth from sheep—and still more from
wolf—we can never hope for full understanding on the part
of any human being. It is a melancholy truth that however
intimate, learned, sympathetic, experienced, sensitive,
penetrating are the friends to whom we look for guidance,
they must always remain just a skin removed: they cannot
quite answer. Not, at any rate, all the time and on every
point. Comprehension comes from God alone. As far as
others are concerned we have always to be making allowances, admitting that we can't find perfect understanding in
them any more than we in our turn can fully satisfy them.

"In that case," it might be asked, "what is the use of asking
advice . . . or giving it?" One is tempted to answer that as
a matter of fact there isn't much, but perhaps it would be
fairer to say that the value of all advice depends upon the
receptivity of the person advised as much as upon the judgement of the person advising. The person who looks for
help from another must preserve an open mind. But not no
mind at all. In the same way the person who does the
advising must be free to sum up the individual case. But not
on the evidence of the case book. The adviser must deal
with the advised as if there was no one else in the world, as
if there existed no recognized method of treatment in "such
cases", as if there had never been any similar situation in
the history of man, as if text-books, formulae, and even
previous experience were as remote as the Himalayas. In
the spiritual life as lived between man and man in the inter-

related existence of the herd the only safe way is to adopt the method of the Good Shepherd Himself. He doesn't deal with His flock but with His sheep. Each one separately. He knows His flock not as a mass-produced assembly but as isolated entities within a body—His body. So we also: our influence will be of use in the world only in the measure that we bring to the problems of others a first-hand and wide-eyed interest. The moment we become doctrinaire we limit the scope of grace. The director who says "Leave this to me: I've met exactly the same thing dozens of times: you've come to the right man" gives himself away at once. Avoid him. He will fit you into a pigeon-hole. He remembers how successful he was with So-and-so. If you remind him of someone else he will treat you as if you were someone else, and that is the last thing a good director will do. A good director will treat you as if there was no one else: he will treat you as being you yourself.

To turn from the director to the soul who asks for direction, it might be added that the scope of grace can also be limited by any attempt at window-dressing. We look for light on *our* problem, not on a coloured problem which bears some resemblance to it. Again sincerity. The unprejudiced approach which is confidently expected from shepherds presupposes a corresponding attitude on the part of the sheep. If a shepherd is under an obligation to provide for the needs of his sheep, there is no less an obligation on the part of the sheep to be sincere about themselves towards their shepherd. "I know mine and mine know me."

BLACK SHEPHERDS OF THE FAMILY

WE LEARN from our Sunday paper that a baby aged two (and black) strayed for a distance of one and a half miles (presumably on all fours) from its home in the heart of Harrisburg, Pa., before it was picked up in the suburbs and returned (calm but protesting) to its parents. We rejoice to find that the pioneer spirit dies hard in Harrisburg, Pa. The incident has far-reaching implications. Is the rising generation to leave its cities with their factories and cinemas, and strike out in the direction of the plains? Does the youth of Harrisburg, Pa., keep late hours?—since it was surely under cover of darkness that our little citizen made such excellent distance. Are we to prepare for a time when whole droves of infants will be seen to leave the shelter of their homes, asserting their independence by forced marches in a body through the streets? Whatever this bold Harrisburg flourish suggests as regards the future, it suggests something very obvious as regards the present: it suggests that its parents don't know how to look after the child.

Of course children can be irritating. Maddening. But it is probably not this that drives a wedge between the mother and her child. Much more often it is something within the parent, not within the child. Fear and laziness are the main obstacles to the harmony of the family: fear of the responsibility which having children involves, and laziness about the work of bringing them up. Parents shrink from having children, or neglect them when they have got them, because they fear the boredom of having to entertain them. But this is by no means the only fear, because people who readily entrust the duty of entertaining their young to a nanny still quake at the idea of another child. There is the financial dread of course, and, for the mother, the physical loathing of pain and all the malaise which precedes the pain; but the main fear is the fear of life: children are a challenge to their parents from the moment of their birth. The sigh of satisfaction at giving birth to a new life is at the same time a sigh of a thousand anticipated anxieties. To some more consciously than to others, but surely in some degree to all, there appear in all their horror or their tedium the demands that must be made upon parenthood. It is difficult to say whether it is the certainties or the uncertainties that make up the greater dread. Perhaps it is easier to face the inevitable question of schooling than the possible question of illnesses, accidents and death. The father and mother see a road of trouble and worry and sorrow and misunderstanding and disappointment stretching out before them . . . "is it worth it?" What they do not see are the rewards. What they do not see either is that *through* the troubles and disappointments and so on come the joys of bringing up a family.

Life in a family is only really successful when everyone has to do a lot of dull things for everyone else. Not heroic things but dull ones. Family life is really only a blue-print of the rest of life: one loves the people one is with, whether they are our parents or our children, not because they are amusing but because they need one to be nice to them. It is when enjoyment without its responsibilities is aimed at that, in the family as in all human relationship, the foundations begin to wobble. The luxury baby who appears in lovely clothes when rung for and who is removed again the moment its mother feels she's had enough is bound to be as insipid a pleasure to a grown woman as an expensive doll. The children that the mother gets on best with are the ones that she has had to do everything for. It is the same old business of the costliness of love. There is no substitute for service, and for a parent to imagine for a moment that he or she can satisfy the parental obligation towards a growing child by giving it money and arranging for entertainments every day of the week is to miss the whole point of its privilege.

The lesson which both children and parents need to learn is that happiness in the family is not the same as being thrilled all day by your family. Naturally one tries to be in good form for the sake of the general harmony, but one must not imagine that for domestic well-being there must be feverish effort—often involving artificial extravagances—to prevent the thing from flagging.

A fear which can induce strain and which certainly can induce suspicion is the parent's dread of being left behind when the son or daughter begins to grow up. It is a very real fear. There is bound to be a gap between two generations, and the feeling that the younger generation will notice it more and more as the years go by makes for a slightly unhealthy desire to cling to a childhood affection long after the time of childhood has passed. The mother who was so enchanted by the confidences and pretty ways of the little boy begins to imagine a falling off in devotion when filial love takes a deeper but outwardly more casual tone. Sometimes of course the fear is justified. More often it is the occasion of mutual misunderstanding. Frequently it leads the disappointed mother to ape the manners of a generation not her own, and this very very seldom goes down.

If parents only trusted their children instead of spoiling them, and if children only leaned on their parents instead of trying to show their independence of them, there would not be all this talk of neglect on the one hand and lack of respect on the other. And at least one problem would cease to vex the guiding minds of Harrisburg, Pa.

MISPLACED PERSONS

THE OTHER day we were told on the wireless—without emotion, and for all the world as if it had been a parliamentary report—that there were no fewer than forty thousand muscles in an elephant's trunk. The announcement was not heralded by any roll of drums, nor was it followed by the usual soft music with which we are familiar as dispelling the sense of anti-climax after news of singular importance. Perhaps somewhere on the world's surface there were pulses that raced and eyes that opened in wonder, but as far as may be judged by the correspondence columns in the press the information was received in silence. But if there are forty thousand muscles in the trunk of an elephant there must be incalculably more influences at work in the personality of a single individual. Consider the complexities of inherited tendency alone, and the elephant's trunk pales into insignificance. Consider the impulses which we have derived, perhaps unconsciously, from the books we have read and the plays we have seen. Consider the fears which date back to the nursery and which have never quite left us, the inhibitions, the shynesses, the instinctive attractions. All these things so mixed up in us, so cut across by what we have learned from others, from experience, from our surroundings, and from the hundred and one apparently fortuitous circumstances of every day, have fitted into the pattern which is *me*. It is idle to speculate what this person, myself, would have become had there been even the slightest disturbance of the contributing causes. But it is not idle to see in the contributing causes the guiding hand of God. That I met a man on the pier at Brighton twenty years ago and picked up from him in ten minutes' conversation a way of looking at suffering is not just an accident: it had been planned by God from all eternity. All day long we are receiving impressions. And transmitting them. On the counter of the soul the merchandise is so varied that we notice only the richer colours and the more expensive materials, but even the lesser wares are entered in the books. This is a thought which can lead to scruple and extravagance, but it is also a thought that can lead to a grateful awareness of the Providence of God.

Take the person who says "if things were different" every time he talks to you about himself. The grievance can apply to the past, the present, and the future. If one's health had only allowed it, if one could count on another two hundred a year, if the war hadn't spoiled it all, if one were ten years younger. So it goes on: each with his image of another self . . . or rather of the same self in a happier setting. Sometimes there is even the delusion that a quite different sphere of activity would make all go well. No, if we could have done better—and by better I mean more good—in another century or on another platform, we may lay a certain bet that God would have so arranged it. We think we would have cut a pretty figure among the martyrs, we envy the chances of the apostles, we look wistfully at the mission fields, the leper colonies, the hermitages in the desert. There is no reality in all this: it is so much cinema stuff. It is not as if the planning of our lives were a haphazard business, as if the time we are expected to spend on earth were tossed into any century, as if our lot were flung anywhere upon the map. There is nothing mistimed or misplaced: our entries fit exactly with our cues, our positions on the stage are allowed for. It is only our acting and our lines that we have to worry about. But note well that ours is a part which no one else can play for us. What by laziness or malice we leave out, what of the idea that exists in the author's mind we twist or travesty, what we cheapen in our greed for applause, what we weaken and flatten by our preoccupation with self, can never be put right again once the curtain has gone down upon the last act. As far as we are concerned the play has a run of only one night. It is a dreadful thing to think of the author in the wings . . . watching the criminal clumsiness, the arrogant stupidity, the exasperating insensitiveness of our performance. He could so easily whisk us off the stage, close the theatre, wash His hands of the whole thing. But instead He is prepared to see His programme wrecked if need be, rather than break the contract of our free will. See what power He puts into the unheeding hands of men. And then we have the effrontery to say "why *this* particular role?" We could have struck finer attitudes in another perhaps, but we could not have had a finer opportunity. "Live conformably to what you are," is an axiom of the schoolmen, "and you will grow." And what is more you will not grow unless you do. We are not given the graces required for growth in any direction other than our own. Before the creation of the world God has thought out the country, class, surroundings, income, relatives, looks and health best suited to the work He wants us to do for Him. Out of millions of years He has chosen *now*. And if the now is so full of mystery and pain that we must cry with Christ, "Father, save me from this hour," at least let us have the faith to go on with the prayer and admit that "for this cause came I unto this hour." This hour is mine, no one else's, and I must not miss it.

WORK

"I'm not in the least interested in my work," is a remark as often heard in the club, the canteen, the common-room, as the remark "we no longer loved one another" is heard in the divorce court. Probably under modern conditions an increasing number of people are bored by their work—just as under modern conditions an increasing number of people are bored by their married lives. But of course nobody ever said that work was going to be all fun. Or married life either. In the sweat of his brow was man told to go about his work. As to how he was to go about his marriage is a question which deserves a separate treatment. Work: sweat.

Nature craves for rest—a rest which fallen nature is obliged to forgo. Or at all events to defer. We pray that eternal rest be granted to the dead. It is the best thing we can think of. Eternal rest and perpetual light. These are the things we know we can never fully enjoy in this life, so we pray that our friends may enjoy them fully in the next. In the meantime there is the business of taking off coats and spitting on hands. There are some—not so many as there used to be, but some—who for one reason or another do not work. They rest. Even in this life they rest. But such is the strangely unpractical joke of nature that their leisure, their envied ease, is almost as great a burden to them as work would have been. Indeed labour is seldom so exhausting as leisure. We look back with loathing to that hour after luncheon when as children we had to rest. That was probably the only time in our lives—apart from periods of convalescence which were just as bad—when we have really

had "time on our hands". And how we longed that someone would come along and take it off. It may require talent
to make a success of work, but it requires genius to make a
success of idleness.

Though work is meant to be an effort it is not meant
to be an agony. In fact it can sometimes be an anodyne.
"I must have something to do . . . anything to take my
mind off it." In sorrow idleness is fatal; occupation is
essential. It seems, then, that we cannot escape the truth that
struggle, and even to a certain extent strain, is necessary to
the general well-being of man. It is part of God's scheme.
And if we look upon labour *only* as a punishment we miss at
least half the point of it. Our work is what we make it:
if we take it up with both hands it can not only be a great
thing to offer to God but it can also be great fun. "Work
out your salvation" says the Bible, not let it come to you as
the result of a single act of faith made from the depths of an
armchair. Life is intended to be a battle—with a battle's
uncertainties, bloodshed, strain, breaking-points, and above
all with a battle's joys. Long before the final victory we
are meant to taste the satisfaction of fighting. It is this
satisfaction, it is these joys, that the world wants to experience without the disgusting necessity of having to fight
for them.

When we begin to wallow in our rest or in our pleasure
we begin also to tire. The battle of life, if we give up
fighting, becomes the most awful bore. Never before has
there been such universal complaint against the dullness
of existence, and yet never before has there been such a
universal attempt to lift the burden of toil from the shoulders
of man. One wonders whether men and women in prim-
itive times suffered from the weariness of having to go on
living . . . or whether the effort to live at all was so
rewarding as to make life worth while. Perhaps if you have

to hunt and fish and dig in order to eat, if you have to learn
the arts of defence, of building, and of cookery in order to
bring up a family, there is less time to think about whether
you find things dull or amusing. On the rare occasions when
a modern man is compelled to fend for himself he finds that
there is a certain pride of achievement in the exercise which
gives an altogether new zest. Probably if we had to defend
our families we would see more point in having them.

The trouble is of course that both our powers and our
tastes are atrophying with disuse. What labour-saving
devices have done in destroying our resourcefulness, ready-
made amusements have done in destroying our faculty of
appreciation. This is particularly the case in the matter of
choosing the way in which we propose to be entertained.
When we look for applied excitement it is obvious that we
shall no longer be satisfied with the surer and more elemental
pleasures. The appetite for truth and beauty will be fobbed
off with cheap sensationalism. Emotions invade the refuges
of the mind, and soon there is nothing but a feverish hunger
for any and every quick-return pleasure that can give some
sort of relief to the nerves. When not in a state of tension,
the mind, with nothing left to fall back upon, is bored.
Solitude, instead of being restful, is unendurable. It is now
that the soul longs to amuse itself and finds it has lost the
power to do so. It has to switch on the wireless instead: a
ready-made entertainment. It has lost the innocent eye of
childhood which sees entertainment everywhere. It has
never had the unsophisticated vision of the worker which
sees interest in doing a job. And once the job has lost its
point, sweat has lost its dignity. The sacredness of Nazareth,
from being the most natural thing in the world, has become
unintelligible. The light, as well as the enjoyment, has gone
out of service.

SERVICE-FLAT CIVILIZATION

IT IS one of the idolatries of the present age to worship physical and material well-being. Granted that man is made for happiness it is just as well that he should know where to look for it. Glamour is so easily mistaken for the real thing. The right kind of joy can be appreciated only by a rightly ordered taste. Children, whose taste is undeveloped, experience great joys. But these are relative joys. Nobody would claim that nursery joys were the highest, or even the keenest. Merely because they are the most innocent they are not necessarily the truest. So for the full appreciation of joy it seems that there has to be some sort of training, some sort of deliberate direction. And the moment we have said this, the whole thing seems to lose point. "If joy isn't spontaneous it is nothing: the fun of it lies in the fact that it's an untutored reaction to a certain kind of stimulus." Quite so—but to what kind of stimulus? Your joy may be as spontaneous as you like, but you must know all about its causes.

Some six hundred years before the coming of Christ an Indian prince arrived at the conclusion that this whole question of joy was so complicated—as being, he held, responsible for the whole question of pain—that the only way out was to eliminate it altogether. Life, decided the Gautama Buddha, was so spoiled by suffering that the less you wanted to live it the better. Do away with joy and you will not want to live it. This bland indifference to human emotion may have a lot to recommend it, but there is no justification for it in the Gospel of Christ. The saint of Christian tradition faces exactly the same problem, and, without a trace of cynicism, goes the first step of the way with Gautama Buddha. "There's a lot of sorrow about . . . it's part of man's make-up to be very largely sad." But this is where he parts company with the Asiatic philosopher. He, the Christian saint, picks up the whole of life with both hands—the pleasures and the pains of it—and makes it into a positive thing. Take St. Francis who embraced equally the beauty of creation and the ugliness of leprosy. Compare him with Buddha who closed his eyes to both. Where one feared joy the other radiated it. Where one, keeping life as far as possible at arm's length, met death in a state of placid boredom, the other, welcoming every moment as it came along, died—despite his blindness, sickness, and poverty—in a state of ecstatic joy.

Thus we get back to the foregoing essay: happiness is to be found in taking trouble, not in evading it. "My yoke is sweet" . . . but how many of us really believe it? How many of us are willing to risk the experiment of seeing whether after all there isn't something rather stimulating about cross bearing? This is where our taste for true joy comes in. No one will say that the joy of, for instance, doing penance for another's sin is the same as the joy of having a hot water bottle in one's bed. But then it requires a rather rare taste to choose to drink of the cup of Christ. We have to buy our joys, and the more we pay for them the better. Man is not born to the appreciation of the highest happiness—any more than he is born to the highest wisdom or skill or holiness—he has to direct himself towards it. Sometimes drag himself towards it. As with knowledge, ability, and sanctity, the understanding of what happiness is all about is arrived at only as the result of search. We speak glibly of a painter's easy line, of a writer's effortless style, of a musician's instinctive touch, but we forget that behind all this is the experience of practice. And not alone

in the arts but in the works of every day there must have
been a corresponding series of renewed efforts, of almost
ascetic training, or refusals to be turned back by opposition
or natural instability, before there can have been any sort of
successful issue. It is the purpose of this essay to show that
success arising from such an expenditure of energy is at-
tended also by perfectly straightforward and highly en-
joyable pleasure. Not merely the pleasure of having brought
off a success, or of having got the thing finished, or of having
beaten someone else, but simply the pleasure which comes
of doing a difficult thing—and your own particular thing—
well. "Ah," you will say, "I do that particular thing well
because I happen to like doing it." Excuse me, but you are
getting the order wrong: you like it because you happen to
have done it well. The point which needs emphasis
here is that we become proficient precisely by working at
it. The pleasure is a by-product. Just as happiness is a by-
product of sanctity. A necessary by-product. "Sorrow,"
says the holy man Job, "does not spring out of the ground."
But then nor does joy. Joy has to be raked out of the embers
of suffering . . . the flower has to be plucked from among
the weeds which threaten it. But we rake the embers not
for the sake of uncovering the joy, we part the weeds not
for the sake of finding flowers. We do these things because
they are our job. Within the ambit of our job are found the
highest and the safest joys—and by "job" I mean not only
our work but our vocation.

To know where to look is the first step towards getting
our joy-values right. But of course we shall probably go
on choosing our hot water bottles.

FRIENDSHIP: THE GENERAL IDEA

CICERO, who wrote a stiffish book about it, defines friendship as "agreement in things sacred and profane, accompanied by goodwill and love". St. Aelred, who enjoyed many and deep friendships, accepts Cicero's definition and adds that for the relationship to be true and lasting it must be cultivated for its own intrinsic worth, the element of self-seeking being eliminated. His, St. Aelred's, great thing is that there can be no genuine friendship between Christians unless Christ comes in to make a third. We shall be borrowing from St. Aelred constantly in this group of essays about friendship because he, more than any writer on the subject, seems to have thought the thing out in a way that has avoided sentimentality on the one hand and severity on the other. You could go through a whole literature on the theme from the works of the saints, and you would find that opinion varies as much as expression; for the purposes of this necessarily slight treatment we can content ourselves with the following quotations.

First by way of reassuring those who think that sanctity is incompatible with human affection we have the words of St. Francis of Sales: "Perfection consists not in having no friendship at all, but in having none except such as is according to God." St. Thomas adds something to this when he says: "Since genuine friendship is founded on virtue, anything good intensifies it . . . perfect friendship cannot extend to many persons." This last observation is perhaps disheartening to those who think that their capacity is inexhaustible. Presumably what St. Thomas means is that though a man may have many true friends he will only once or twice in a lifetime know the joy of perfect friendship.

Of its nature it must be more rare than love. Many are called but few are chosen: few are so tuned by grace and temperament as to merit the title which St. Thomas reserves for them. Cassian is equally emphatic about the necessity of having one's foundations right in this matter of friendship: "Friendships begun without a desire for perfection," he says, "cannot long preserve their unity unbroken."

Thus we get this: God is the basis of all love, and is therefore the source of true friendship. Charity, whatever form it takes, is expansive. It communicates what is best in the soul, and invites a corresponding return. The relationship which results is not an end in itself but a means: it can advance the holiness of both parties. Where this exists in its finest form there is no room for self-seeking: all the purely human element is sublimated in the search for God. It is this that is more rare than love. "Such friendship," says one of the characters in St. Aelred's Dialogue, "is not for all." Dare any of us say that we possess the singlemindedness, the disinterestedness, the spirituality of such an approach? Probably not, but at least it gives us the line which we are expected to go upon. If we master the outline there is always the hope that we shall be able to fill it in with a practice not altogether out of keeping with the theory. With the nature of Christian friendship established, we can now get on with the less boring question as to what are the requirements of the Christian friend.

In the first place it is not to be supposed that two people can be friends on the lines indicated above unless they have had time to see what the thing means and to get into the way of living it. The writers on friendship are inclined to begin at the wrong end, painting a picture of an ideal relationship which it may have taken years to bring about. This is profoundly discouraging to someone who knows that he has not the same purity of intention about his affection and so is forced to the melancholy conclusion that his is no true friendship. In the actual fact there are probably no friendships, or at all events very few, that *start off* with the idea of mutual sanctification in view. They start off by mutual attraction. There is nothing wrong in this; it is perfectly natural that they should. It is only when the friendship has got going—when the partners in the affair can now turn round and see that they are no longer mere acquaintances—that there arises the question of abiding by certain sanctions and of giving the thing a certain direction. Granted, then, that on the negative side there is nothing wrong about the friendship to begin with, and on the positive side that one wants to make of it something pleasing to God, what are the qualities that one looks for in this person who is coming to mean more and more in one's life, and who looks as if he is going to stay?

Must he share my tastes, my interests, my choice of other people? I don't think so. He must sympathise with them and tolerate them, but it will be enough if he shares my enthusiasms and loyalties. I don't ask that he should understand the things that I like but I insist that he should understand my liking them. His principles must be my principles but I can't see that his appreciations need be mine; it will help, though, enormously if they are. What is more important than having the same likes and dislikes is having absolutely no secrets about them. Once a friend begins to hide anything, the chances are that the foundations will begin to crack. This is both the condition and the effect of friendship, that there should be nothing furtive, nothing kept back, nothing which is feared might shock. I must trust my friend sufficiently to let him see the flaws in my composition. If I don't do this I am expecting him to make a friend of someone whom he does not know: I am asking to be liked for what I appear to be on the surface: I am acting under false pretences, attracting him with a borrowed bait. Besides seeing my weaknesses and putting up with my failures this friend of mine must be ready also to look for any good that there may be in me: he must accept, in other words, what I have to offer. If a friend refuses to be advised, it means that the partnership is so onesided that it isn't a question of partnership at all but of patronage. The whole point of a union is that one cannot stand alone but that the goods of each are enjoyed together.

From what has been said it might be thought that for a friendship to flourish there should be incessant exchanges of confidence, of advice, of innermost manifestations. Not at all. The fewer declarations there are, the better. A friendship can suffer, like so many things, from over exposure. The resources are liable to drain away if there is too much of the heart-to-heart. I am only saying that the mutual trust, the readiness to lean and be leant on, the openness about oneself must be *there*—not that they must constantly be drawn upon. The trouble is that some rather timorous and insecure people imagine that they have to show their trust and reveal their consciences in order to prove the quality of their faith. This is a misconception. The virtues attaching to friendship are for help and not for luxury: they are to be taken for granted, and not trotted out for fun or reassurance. There may never be occasion to call upon them at all; there is certainly never occasion—save when they bear directly upon the issue—to talk about them. Votes of confidence are always tricky things to handle, declarations of affection still more so. Often it is found that on the plea of putting all the cards on the table it is only the one suit—hearts—that has been played. It has been made an excuse to wallow. Wallowing does no friendship any good; in fact it wrecks it. Sentiment spoils everything, and even the toughest of us are regrettably mawkish underneath. All this must be kept

well down. Apart from the fact that these declarations
which we have mentioned are a voiced weakness where
there should be silent strength, there is the additional
disadvantage that the disclosure, once made, leaves little
else to talk about. This is bad. Friends should not be
reduced to having only their relationship as a topic; interest
in other things should increase and not wane as a result of
their association, and if their main subject of discussion is
each other, the whole thing becomes insipid and enfeebled.
There must be a strict austerity about friendship or it will
leave the wrong taste. Sacrifice and not satisfaction is the
expression of love, and the willingness to sacrifice the
satisfaction of expressing affection is one of the highest and
hardest forms the sacrifice can take. Friends should be
prepared to forgo the gratification of either giving or
demanding evidence. The deep things in man are often
best safeguarded by the most obstinate dumbness. It is part
of the price he has to pay for possessing them.

If we have been here considering that form of friendship
which veers towards the romantic it is not because it is the
most sacred or the most profane, but simply because it is
the most in need of getting right. The straightforward
unemotional kind more or less runs itself, and you don't
have to be told to be tough about it. Its dangers are of
a more bluff order: irritation, neglect, irresponsibility, un-
accommodating insistence upon getting one's own way.
But where possible sloppiness comes in, the matter has to be
treated with greater delicacy. Though with no less firmness.
There is a sediment in the heady wine which must not be
allowed to rise to the surface. The vintage which has been
laid down in heaven and decanted on earth is so rare and
precious that nothing may be risked.

FRIENDSHIP: SOME FURTHER ASPECTS

WE HAVE seen that Cicero's agreement in things sacred and profane implies harmony of principle rather than identity of interest. But there is more to it than this: it is not just something which, having arisen out of a natural and spiritual conformity, is there for ever. It is not a lump sum out of heaven with no liabilities. There must be the will to preserve that harmony against disturbance from without and decay from within. And to preserve it for good. "He that is a friend," says the Book of Proverbs, "loveth at all times." All times. Not when it suits him or when there is nothing to prevent it, but when he feels the thing to be crumbling, when he is puzzled by the behaviour of his friend, when other people oppose the relationship, when everything seems to conspire to break the thing up, when he sees the obstacles in their starkest form, when he has been treated abominably or casually or maddeningly . . . these are the times when his loyalties must remain fixed and unquestioning. Patience has a boring sound about it, but in one form or another it is patience—call it constancy, longsuffering, magnanimity, or simply generosity—that is friendship's particular virtue. Heroic endurance is sometimes required to put up with the misunderstandings of what is accepted as an understanding alliance. But this is quite as it should be. Our loves ought to cost us mo than our hates. One of the saddest things in life is to watch the inability of one or other in a friendship to meet the price which his privilege demands. The partnership dissolves, and instead of Cicero's agreement of two and Aelred's three-sided communion of which Christ is a member, there

is estrangement and sometimes even enmity. The good
that could have come of it is wasted; there is a gap in the
scheme of God; two people are missing something which
would have given them happiness as well as sympathy.
"Friendship that can cease," says St. Jerome rather fiercely,
"was never friendship." Wasn't it? At all events it might
have been.

The trials which some friendships have to endure can
bring things to the potential breaking point—perhaps if
the friendship is to be of the highest order *have* to bring
things to the potential breaking point—before matters settle
down again and everything goes on smoothly. Disappointment, separation, and even such a maddeningly silly
thing as a piece of malicious gossip, can go far towards
upsetting the balance. Richard Rolle is comforting here
when he says, speaking of one man's disillusion in the face of
another's failure, "For no error can the friendship be broken,
since if it be true friendship the friend will be all the more
busy to call him back again that erred." Indeed this might
be taken as a test: is he prepared to begin again after what he
has seen, and to extend the same confidence as before? Not
merely forgiveness but confidence. "It is more difficult to
restore faith than create it," says Disraeli. If the difficulty is
overcome on the one side by renewing the trust, it is overcome on the other by rising to meet it.

As well as unshakable faith there must be among friends
a large indifference or incupidity. Disinterested must be
their attitude. Friendship (like virtue and bridge when not
played for money) is its own reward. Nothing is to be got
out of it but itself. That will be quite enough, and if we
look for the pleasures it affords we cheapen it at its source.
St. Bernard is particularly strong on this point. "The reward
of friendship," he says, "is its enjoyment . . . it is suspect
when upheld by the thought of gaining something else."

St. Augustine says much the same, pointing out that whereas we readily and rightly despise as mercenary the affection which looks for gain from a friend, we forget that it is much the same thing to look for expressed affection from him. "Friendship should be gratuitous," he concludes, "a friend should be loved freely for himself and not for anything else."

Lastly (and briefly, since this point has been touched upon elsewhere in these pages) there must be no cutting off of other contacts as a result of forming one rather closer one. There must be nothing all-absorbing, exclusive, enclosed. A holy man once told me that he liked to think of himself as being a piece of bark flung into a pond, and that various kinds of fish could come and nibble at him whenever they liked. "Every now and again God sends a goldfish and then it's very jolly and one gives thanks for it, but of course the point is that one's there for whatever comes along." This is surely the answer, provided the presence of the goldfish is not allowed to scare away the others.

FRIENDSHIP: THE TRANSITION PERIOD

"IT IS a terrible thing," says Oscar Wilde, "to bid farewell to those whom one has known for a very short while." It seems that there is something about new and untried friends that outweighs what we enjoy about those that have stood the test of time. A new person is like a new tune: we like it, however unsatisfactory, better than a classic. This looks all wrong, of course, put in such terms but it works out quite correctly in the long run. Either the acquaintance becomes a friend or he doesn't. If he does, we were right to like him from the beginning; if he doesn't, we go on liking the classics.

We needn't feel the least guilt at having been attracted by the superficial, by what we have no real knowledge of. We have not had a chance of being attracted by anything else. In the forming of a friendship it is not the superficial *as* the superficial that appeals; it appeals because it is on top and so appears first. It is natural and right that a person should feel drawn towards what looks to him like a pleasant character; for one thing he wouldn't otherwise be drawn at all, and for another he is, perhaps unconsciously, going ahead of what he sees to what he hopes and expects will be there. The quality that we call charm in people is hardly ever a stop-short thing, it is the agreeableness that is the promise of a good deal more beyond. Human nature seldom falls under the spell of an enchantment which holds out nothing but the immediate moment. Discovery, whether of people or places or books or things, is the kind of ecstasy which is at least equal parts anticipation. It opens up possibilities of further discovery.

Right. Acquaintanceship has developed along the right lines into easy fellowship. On both sides general impressions have been verified. Each enjoys the other's company and the good qualities of both are far more in evidence than the bad. In fact the bad qualities are not in evidence at all. It is not that either is putting on an act to deceive the other—conscious insincerity is probably never dreamed of—nor is it that their regard for each other blinds them to each other's faults—friends are not like lovers in this respect—it is simply that the good is shown to such advantage that the rest is not taken into account. The bad might just as well not be there. For practical purposes it isn't. This is one of the strongest arguments in favour of friendship, that even in the early stages it brings out the best in people and not the worst. There is nothing self-conscious or priggish about this: it is only because they are necessarily in good form when they meet, and that therefore the unamiable elements in their natures are in abeyance. The situation now is that the two do a lot of laughing and talking; they never feel bored; they learn—without the conversation ever becoming particularly personal or intimate—a great deal about each other; their lives receive an impetus which they are aware of and which adds enormously to their usefulness as well as to their good spirits; the whole thing *without being in the least sentimental* (yes, the italics here are important) is a highly stimulating and amusing adventure. There is no harm in all this—the worst that can be said about it is that there has probably been a good deal of time wasted in perfectly innocent but entirely idle discussion—the only thing is that there has been nothing yet to test the real nature of the relationship. So far it has been a delightful experience, an irresponsible interlude.

How long does this state of affairs last? There can be obviously no generalization, and the question is an idle one anyway. The point is that it won't last and isn't meant to. "There doesn't seem to be the same sparkle . . . I seem to have got duller . . . why can't it be on the same terms as when it started? . . . I must be very fickle." So run the thoughts sooner or later of the person who would never admit that he was disappointed in his friend but who can't help finding that he is disappointed in his friendship. On both sides flatness is felt to have set in. Any attempt to jolly things up is felt to be forced. Which, indeed, it is. Conversation becomes a strain; silence becomes awkward. This is the point at which many friendships disintegrate; these are the lean months. But now precisely is the time to hang on. Now is the time to recognize the fact that not only has the relationship entered upon a new phase—this is all too clear—but that it is a necessary one and—if only the two parties will be sensible about it—a temporary one.

In the nature of the case there can't be the same enter-tainment-content as there was at the beginning. The engaging manner, or rather the novelty of it, which each one appreciated at the beginning has begun to wear thin. The originality which was in a large measure the attraction has lost its edge; the amusing reminiscences are coming round for the second time; letters are getting more laboured and less frequent; there is none of the carefree abandon about meetings and no particular sense of wrench about partings. The same thing happens, exactly, at a certain stage in married life. All it means is that the first stock has been exhausted and there is a lull before the reserves are ready to be drawn upon. The tragedy is so often that this lull, whether in married life or in the unfolding of a friendship, is taken to be the infallible sign that the thing has become unstuck. Unstuck for good.

Not only in human intercourse is there this conviction that the fire has burnt itself out: the same can happen in a soul's relationship with God. What we have to convince ourselves of in each case is that there has *got* to be this interim period before one set of conditions has been fully exchanged for another. Where the spiritual life is concerned we have God dictating the terms of the new relationship, and until these are understood there is the state of insufficiency which is called the Night of the Senses. It is during this transitional phase that the faculties are being trained to a more subtle, more deep, more real perception. Powers used to one mode of operation are told to forget their previous knowledge and adapt themselves to a new activity. The love which results from this painful and bewildering process is incomparably more pure, more solid, more self-sacrificing than anything that went before.

In the world of human affairs it is the same. Friendship dictates its terms, and until the old conditions are left behind the new ones cannot be realized. It is in the interval that the new language must be learned. The bond which results will, again, be incomparably more sure and unselfish than whatever it was that acted as a link in the beginning. The enduring qualities have been picked up. Everything is now very real and mellow and open. There have been readjustments to meet the needs of temperament, there have been sacrifices to mood and taste, angularities have been discovered and made allowance for. The course is smoother than it has ever been. The affair, at long last, has slid into position. This is the normal, the true, the appropriate. Nothing has been lost to the original conception except such non-essentials as it can do better without. Much has been gained in their place. There is now an understanding that is more far-reaching, an admiration that is better founded. It is an altogether satisfactory condition to be in.

"But why, if it is all to come to nothing," you may
ask, "should the first part feel as real as it does? Why
don't these things move on progressively from the start
without such misleading introductions? It means one
wants to compare the present with the past . . . and the
past appears in such a far more satisfactory light." The
first part *is* real. Its reality need never be repudiated for
a moment. But so is a sunrise real. The radiance of dawn
is true enough but transitory: it leads on to the less spectacular heat of day. The introduction shouldn't be misleading.
Without the early adventure of friendship you would never
find within you enough of the exploring spirit to carry you
on to the serious business of discovering things that are even
more worth while than what was revealed in the introduction. Again the best illustration of this is to be found in
marriage, where there has to be the falling in love or there
would not be sufficient material to carry the weight of
married life. The danger lies in mistaking the earlier stages
for the permanent thing, and it is probably because people
have never learned from their friendships what they were
meant to learn that marriages go wrong. Obviously if
you have never done anything but flit from friend to
friend, lifting the icing and leaving the cake, you will not
know what to look for when it comes to the more irrevoc-
able union. When the icing is finished, you will not know
what to do with the cake; and there won't be anything
else to eat. Perhaps God gives the grace of friendship that
man may value the sacrament of matrimony.

GENEROSITY

ONE OF the complaints against God is that He seems to leave so much of the work to us. The duties of religion are felt to be a burden which we can just endure, but which we cannot endure with any show of gladness. There is not much margin. We can't be jolly and generous about it. And yet God expects "good measure and running over"— generosity flowing from the heart of a cheerful giver. Conscious of always pressing uphill on flat tyres we feel disappointed at the lack of hilarity in our service. We admire the hearty gaiety of the Psalmist but we are seldom able to share his mood. Probably the reason for this is that we are used to thinking that religion is boring while we are not used to thinking that we are boring. We are evidently so boring, however, that when faced with nothing but our own selves on our lonely way to God we are bored stiff. And we put the blame on religion. It is only fortunate that God does not find our service as boring as we do. But you can see why all this calls for generosity on our part: first of all generosity towards God in giving Him the benefit of the doubt and assuming that the insufficiency is on our side, and secondly generosity in the service which we owe Him, giving gladly what we admit to be at best an indifferent work.

The average Catholic (if such a person exists) contents himself with giving God His due. For him the virtue of justice is the limit of his endeavour: justice towards God and man. Very good. But not superlatively good. Not good enough, anyway, for the saints. Generosity begins for them where justice leaves off. Generosity comes along and says: "While we are about it, let's make a thing of it." After all the Gospel invites us to this. Love is positive. The Gospel does not tell us what we have to do to avoid going to hell, it tells us what we have to do in order to love God. So long as religion means to us a negative thing, a list of prohibitions, it must continue to be a bore. Once we see it as opening out a wealth of possibility we glimpse the true purpose of life. The purpose of life is not boring.

How many shrink from investigating the possibility of closer relationship with God in the fear "lest having Him we have nought else beside". Such a fear can only mean that we regard Christ as so jealous a God that no joy may linger in the heart that is consecrated to Him. Which is nonsense. Christ came to direct the heart of man, not to destroy it. Christ came that we might share His life, not that we should impoverish our own. To conceive of sanctity as a damping down process, a gradual reduction of the human element, is to miss the whole point of the thing. The Gospel is explosive, dynamic, life-giving. The Sacraments are vitalizing, expansive, positive. There is nothing quiescent about Christianity. It is a leaven which bubbles up, a seed which presses to the surface. Unless the members of the Church are prepared to give to religion—I am not speaking now of giving in money—they have no right to complain that they are getting very little out of it. But it is just those who are the sleeping partners in the relationship with God who do so complain. The generous are too generous to mind what they get. And incidentally of course they get far more than they would have ever thought of bargaining for.

Generosity generates generosity. It is one of those laws. You give, and are never out of pocket. In fact you are the richer for giving. So is everyone else. Charity —which is another word for generosity as well as being another word for love—broadcasts charity. It evokes it as well, but for the moment we can consider it as expending rather than as inviting. It is like wisdom: imparted and not merely transferred. No loss is sustained by giving either love or knowledge. Generosity leaves no hollow as if you had taken a spoonful from a pudding and given it to another. The giving of love is like the giving of information: another has what only one had before. You tell a man the time, or the way to the Underground, or how to judge a horse, and there is no vacancy in your mind as the result. You do not say: "Now I shall have to guess the time . . . buy a map . . . pick a horse at random." Christ, from the store of His infinite wisdom, gave information. But what was even more important He gave love. He gave Himself. He gave all. This is what we call generosity. He communicated Himself to man. He does it every day at the altar . . . inviting us to do the same.

We talk of the "common fund" of Christianity and perhaps our mind jumps uneasily to the thought of Peter's Pence or the African Mission. But of course the common fund is another term for the Mystical Body. It is a fund that may be exhausted of material possessions while it grows in spiritual ones. The body feeds, but the food is not destroyed. The body sleeps, but the time is not wasted. So charity—whether work for God or for souls—is never a drain upon our spiritual powers, it is always an increase. Not only is this true in the supernatural order of grace but even in the natural order of human happiness. It is the expansive, outgoing, hospitable people who are the happiest. Why? Not, as might be imagined, because of the moral glow which must come from having added to the sum of general wellbeing, but simply because it is in the nature of

man to be communicative. Eden was intended to be the
garden of love, the home of generosity. Gethsemane, the
second garden of love, is still the market-garden of generosity. Humanity was generous enough before the fall, and
since the Redemption it has been re-deemed worthy of
being generous again.

DEATH: OTHER PEOPLE'S

WE CAN read about death, meditate upon it, sympathize with those who have suffered its losses even prepare ourselves when we see it coming to someone we care for, but always death catches us on the wrong foot. We know when we have watched someone die that death is something quite apart, that each death is a unique event like falling in love, and that its pain cannot be reconciled to what we know about it. Death escapes theory. Or rather it is so blinding that the theory means nothing. Oh yes, we believe that the departed soul is happier now than it ever was when we knew it; we know that our relationship is not at an end and that we shall enjoy the other's company more satisfactorily in heaven than we have ever done on earth; we accept the fact that God has judged it better from everyone's point of view—the soul's, ours, His own—that this life should cease at this particular time. We assent to all this but it doesn't make the smallest difference. Reason says Yes, habit says Thy will be done, but I—the me whom the departed soul has known and loved and eaten with and laughed at—say No, I refuse it, it's beyond my power to accept.

This apparent rebellion is, to the well-intentioned Christian who is trying to see God's will in everything that happens, disturbing beyond words. Is it, he asks himself, that my sorrow is sweeping me away from God? Does the pain I feel show my affection to be too human, too little related to God? Has the time of my spiritual training been so ineffectual that when a first-class personal grief comes crashing into my life I have nothing but a few dry texts

with which to meet it? And thus the soul concludes that
there has been self-deception all along, and that its service
of God has been a papery thing unable to stand up against
the weight of affliction, and that loving God's creatures so
much it has loved God Himself all too little.

It is at this point that the soul must pull itself together or
it will suffer a worse evil than that of loss, it will suffer the
bitterness of disillusion. It must tell itself that far from
being shocked at the wealth of its feeling it should be glad
of it. Not for a moment should it wallow in its agonies—
that would be to pull the whole thing down—but it should
realize that there is a reason for the upset. The soul is *meant*
to feel these things. And feel them very deeply indeed.
For some more than others, but for all of us at times, there
is need to be reminded of our humanity. And there is
nothing like the loneliness which follows the death of
someone we love to do this for us. Perhaps in our pursuit
of the supernatural we have forgotten about the natural.
Death brings it back to us with cruel force. In our way to
God there must be nothing left out: the human emotions,
purified and strengthened, must be brought along. Turning
our lives outside in, death comes to teach us the lesson of the
Incarnation, and we remember that as Christ is human so
are we. Perhaps we have so sedulously contemplated His
divinity that we have forgotten His humanity. The Word
was made flesh; the body died and rose again. By the death
of another we learn more of Christ: by the life of Christ
we learn the meaning of another's death.

We are always liable to make the mistake of driving
a wedge between God's spiritual and God's natural order.
We are tempted to confuse the natural with the carnal.
Consequently when we see in ourselves a human affection
we measure it against our love of God, and draw the worst
conclusions. But love, rightly ordered, is a coat without

seam: it is we who make of it a thing of parts. With those in whom love of God and love of man work together as they are meant to work, there cannot be that sense of helplessness which overcomes us when one or other consolation is withdrawn. It is only where the balance of charity is uneven that the suffering in one renders the other comfortless. Another's death should leave us sad, yes, but not at sea in our sadness. And even in saying this we seem to be dragging in a theory to fortify ourselves against the poignancy of grief. Is the only consolation then—for those who dare not claim that the scales of charity are truly adjusted—an abstract one? A piece of knowledge and not a refuge?

What is it that hurts when we see our friends die? It is not the will that suffers, but the heart and mind. In a way we could never have foreseen or provided against, we see how utterly we are cut off from the personality of the dead. It is not that we feel cut off from the bigger spiritual relationship which can survive death but rather from the hundred and one lesser links which go to bind people together—those incidental things which when looked back upon seem of enduring significance but which were taken so much for granted at the time. We become suddenly aware—though we would have known all along if we had thought about it—that we can never again get in touch with, for instance, the other person's sense of humour, with his prejudices, his appreciations, his moods. All that has gone. We know that for the rest of our lives we shall do without his mannerisms, his shyness, his ways of pronouncing things. The voice is silent—yes, we had expected it would be—but that the yawns and sudden bursts of laughter will never be repeated is almost more than we can bear. It is realizations of this sort that make all deaths sudden deaths. And it is realizations of this sort that lead us back again to the belief that we are being horribly selfish: what we hate is having to give up *all*. If we cling so closely to the things that do not matter, how inordinate must our clinging have been to the things that do? But this argument is not quite fair; there is a less condemning explanation. If we take our memories back to those occasions we have instanced—those moments which were hardly noticed at the time but which seem charged with meaning now—we shall see that they were not passing moments at all but that they had something in them of eternity. They have stood the test of time because they happen to be everlasting. They were so true that not even our memories could blunt their edge or falsify them. To have enjoyed in this way is not to have enjoyed selfishly, it is to have enjoyed rightly. It means that our enjoyment has come from others and from God. Which is where enjoyment is meant to come from. It is precisely because God is Love that love's moments, however insignificant they seem at the time, are everlasting. Recollections which stab us and then are gone again are not just momentary returns of momentary experiences, they are fragments of eternity. Human love, since it is in part divine, is not mortal merely; love is essentially immortal, but because it is enjoyed by beings that are mortal it can be realized only intermittently. In moments. It is the momentary aspect of our affection that makes us think it has been selfish; it is its immortality that tells us how—in origin and end at all events—it is divine.[1]

[1] Some of the above has appeared, though in an altered form, in my book *Ezechiel: Man of Signs.*

DEATH: OUR OWN

DEATH, as a subject for meditation, is right out of fashion. There was a time when no retreat giver or spiritual writer would dream of leaving it out of his programme. But all that has changed, and now death is lucky if it gets a passing mention. I was once entertained to luncheon at a Carmelite friary where it is the custom during meals of silence to have a skull upon the table. The religious, while they are eating, dwell upon the thought of death. On the day that I was there, the prior decided to relax the rule of silence in my honour—an act of courtesy towards the Benedictines—and the following ceremony took place. A sign was given; the brethren stopped eating; a lay brother advanced up the refectory; the skull was picked up, put in a cardboard box, removed to a window-sill . . . and the community broke into gentle chatter. So with the whole question of death: it has been put away for another time.

Perhaps one reason why death does not go down with this generation is that it went down so very well with the last. It was treated in such a highly imaginative way—people glowed over it—that we of a more hardbitten period feel slightly ashamed of the whole subject. We are not as simple as our fathers were, and the deathbed scenes which excited and appalled in days gone by bring not a tingle to the modern scalp. Perhaps this is no bad sign. Death—our own anyway—must not be wailed over. The imagination is no weapon with which to fortify ourselves against the horrors of death. The sinister image which stalks, macabre and threatening, through our prayers can well be replaced by something more true and certainly more jolly. We can envisage the reality of death all the more surely because the less fervidly. We should never get worked up about anything—least of all about death.

Life is the thing to worry about, if anything is, not death. Death is a detail. Death is nothing more than changing gear in the journey of life. Sin stops the journey; death doesn't. It is because people have mistaken ideas of life that they get the wrong idea of death. They look upon life as a wireless battery getting weaker and weaker until it finally runs out. It would be more true to think of it as an inexhaustible battery surviving the rest of the apparatus. Death is the point at which the casing is found to be too worn out to contain the spirit which it harbours. A new sphere has to be found for the spirit's activity. Corruption cannot possess incorruption; mortality has to put on immortality. Death is simply the switch over.

We are like the men in Gedeon's army: we bear the flame of life sheltered in earthenware vessels. At the sound of the trumpet the covering will crack and fall away; the flame will shine in its proper element. We don't really know what life can be like until the covering falls away and we die.

Eternal life is not strictly *another* life, a different kind of thing, an altogether new existence unrelated to what has gone before: it is a new mode of continuing the same life— under vastly different conditions. Reward and punishment are not to be regarded as unconnected effects—in the way that a silver cup is a prize, or a fine is a penalty—but rather as part of a necessary sequence—where the prize for success is full enjoyment of that in which success has been won, and the penalty frustration of the powers misused.

Seen in such terms it is clearly a mistake to attend to the question of death at the expense of the question of life. If in life we are facing the right way, we are not going to be twisted round at the moment of death. All the same, you will say, there is the grim inevitableness of death—not only that it is rolling towards me at this moment and is bound to arrive one day, but that having arrived there's no second chance, no further appeal. Quite so, but there is nothing very terrifying about that. If death is an enemy, Christ has triumphed over it. We don't trust in our merits but in His. As far as we can we insure ourselves against final loss, but the policy which we take out in our own name doesn't cover everything. Christ's Passion does. He has given us the victory.

Even the physical shrinking from the act of death need not worry us. *Now*, while in full health, of course we shrink: death is not natural to us. But it will be natural to us then. When the time comes and our energies have slowed down and the soul is ready to leave the body it will seem the most obvious thing in the world. We shall probably welcome the idea of the change, and even long for it.

The patriarch Jacob had no love for the land of Egypt. To the Israelite it spelled mystery and menaced suffering. So it was with a very natural dread that Jacob received his son's invitation to journey south and cross the border from the country which had been his home for a hundred years. That he shrank from the change and had misgivings about it is not to be wondered at, but when it came to the point and he saw Joseph coming to meet him with his retinue of attendants at Egypt's boundaries, the old man wept for joy. Joseph who had gone before him into the dreaded land was alive and had come to fetch him. That was all that mattered: everything would be well. For us there is a greater than Joseph who has gone away and come to life again. When we see Him coming to meet us with His friends shall we hesitate?

PRAYER: A QUESTION OF ANGLE

A soul may regard his daily period of prayer from one of two points of view: either as being the time which generates the spiritual energy which is to be distributed over the rest of the day, or as being the one time when the rest of the day can be forgotten and when there is nothing to worry about but loving God. The first makes prayer a sort of marshalling yard or clearing house where the soul sits issuing instructions, reports and material; where it gets its ideas sorted out, its strategy co-ordinated, its forces assembled, its despatches draughted . . . before rolling up its sleeves and getting down to work. The other view makes prayer a much less busy, but no less difficult, affair of trying to express adoration. Both views may be right; it is merely a question of which obtains the better results—better from God's point of view, of course, not better in the sense of more recognisable from ours. It is only suggested here that since our life is a thing to be unified and not divided, the aim should be to find a prayer-motive which simplifies rather than multiplies and splits up. The more direct the approach the better, and since we come to the business of prayer by an angle anyway—because the union with God cannot be immediate—it will help enormously if the angle is not further complicated by other angles.

Our work, our recreation, our prayer, our reading, our thought should emerge in the day as a single whole rather than as separate entities strung together by the coupling force of prayer. On this showing, the second and simpler view has more to recommend it, so it seems to me, than the first. If you take the first view it rather implies that you must make your half hour (or however long it is that you spend in prayer) a rattling success or the rest of the day will be lost to God. Whereas the purpose of prayer is not success as we measure it, not efficiency, but love. It suggests also that you get up from your knees at the end of it saying: "Well, that's over, and now for the next thing." Whereas prayer, as we have been insisting in these pages is not so much an exercise as a life, not a series of more or less related acts so much as a constant getting near to God. Certainly this will require the exercise of repeated acts, but the acts will tend to become closer and closer related until they merge into one another and cover the whole range of the soul's outward and inward activity. The expression of this prayer will of course be intermittent——because it is not in the power of man to apply his mind to God all day—but when it is expressed it will be found to take a singularly unelaborate form. So long as it expresses a desire to love and not to stop loving, it can be as wordless, imageless, idea-less as you like.

Of the two ways of approach, this, the second one, gives us a balanced progression of inward and outward activity: our prayer becomes the fruit of our lives, our lives become the fruit of our prayer. The one feeds the other. If you take the first—the storing up energy—approach, the process works in one direction only: prayer becomes the preparation for action.

But whichever way the soul looks at it, the goal and not the approach is what matters. Let a soul get to God by any means he can; I am only saying that for most people the way is made too elaborate and complicated—with the result that unless one is conscious the whole time of making a quantity of acts one judges the prayer to have been a failure. The slowing down of talk is a good sign, not a bad one. "Not in much speaking" does true prayer consist says our Lord. In the same way our ideas should become fewer, our imaginations less detailed. As the soul grows more used to divine love there is, as there is in the case of human love, less to talk about, less to engage the speculative and imaginative faculties. We become lovers and not talkers or thinkers. What conceptions we have in prayer are not new and so not very exciting, our imagery is filed down, our idiom reduced to words of one syllable, even our needs and resolutions are confined to expressing our primary need for God and our fixed resolve to love Him better. In proportion as we grow less interested in ourselves and more interested in God, our own side of the thing is less discussed, less dramatised, less worried about. We become less self-conscious. We become more and more conscious that the only thing to worry about is God, and that whatever we have to say to Him can be summed up very simply. Sometimes with no more than a look. Prayer goes up the scale of the faculties: we begin by expressing our love in vocal prayer, which is the use of the senses; we go on then to meditations and considerations, which is the use of imagination; the next step is in the will, and for this there is no need for form or phrase. Colloquies give place to acts, acts to affections, affections to the prayer of simple regard or loving presence. God is the centre, and our lives rather than our sentiments are wrapped round Him. He is all and nothing else is of any consequence.

YOUTH

W HEN Y O U T H is written of or spoken about, it is almost invariably eulogised. Here, for a few brief pages, it is going to be attacked. Not that there is anything particularly wrong with being young—any more than there is anything particularly right. In itself the thing is neutral. Each stage in our lives is what we make it, and though youthfulness is no nobler or more base than either babyhood or old age there is this about it that its energies make for greater effects than do either the embryo forces of the baby or the spent vitality of the octogenarian. We see youth in all its splendour as something essentially golden and glorious. We must beware of deception on this point. Middle age can do just as well. Physically youth looks better, and so wins all the applause, but morally there's nothing in it. More gilded is youth than middle age, but not necessarily more golden. How easily are our eyes deceived by glamour. The powers of youth can work both ways.

For the last twenty years or so, youth has had it all its own way. But marching before the band, striking attitudes upon the pedestal, receiving the helm with open hand are danger-ous occupations. Dangerous, I mean, to one's humility. And youth, as the result of the process, has grown arrogant. It might have sat back and grown soft—which in some ways would have been worse—but it hasn't, it has grown asser-tive. It is not the fault of youth that this has happened, it is the fault of the generation before—it is our fault. We, the middle aged, must take the blame. To honour unduly anything which has only relative value is always bound to have evil consequences, and this is what we have done with regard to youth. We have done the same with regard to physical fitness: the body, at all events in some countries, has taken the place which belongs to the soul. It is the old story of nature wanting to be super-nature—but without the assistance of grace. Youth then, in its search for further inspiration, has looked in the wrong direction for its ideals. That this has happened is hardly surprising when we consider that there weren't many people of the foregoing generation who were pointing in the right direction. It would be fanciful, but not strictly accurate, to say that flattery had quite literally turned youth's head; it would be more honest, and more true, to say that youth grew tired of being guided by weak-kneed guides and so looked for more stimulating leadership elsewhere. Experimenting in paganism, youth found in Race and Force what it had failed to find in Christianity. It found what we of the older generation had failed to *show* of Christianity. There was nothing wrong with Christianity: it was we, the weak-kneed Christians, who were wrong. And there were one or two things about paganism which happened to be right; it was youth—questing, experimenting youth—which happened to find them out. This the leaders of the new paganism were not slow to exploit. The Gospel of Christ was losing its appeal . . . right! a new gospel must be substituted. Let us, said the gods of the new paganism, stick to some of the old virtues; let us retain what must always appeal to youth of every age . . . let us call for sacrifice . . . for generosity . . . for hardness. Let us be tough.

And so the enthusiasm which had once been harnessed to the Gospel came to be diverted, pledging itself to the service of a fabricated ideal. It was our fault; we had let the moment slip. Instead of asking for heroism we had gone about saying that religion wasn't really so bad after all. We had laid so much stress on the sweetness of the yoke that the yoke itself hardly appeared worth worrying about. We handled the Crown of Thorns so gingerly that no one was allowed to feel the spikes. We may have preached Christ, but we didn't preach Christ crucified—or if we did, we omitted to preach Christians crucified too. The fault with us was that we didn't give a *lead*—or if we did, we drew the spotlight upon our own claims to leadership instead of pointing to the only possible Leader, Christ. Surely that was one of the mistakes of the last twenty years—looking upon Our Lord as a figure to be honoured and studied only and not also to be introduced into everyday life and followed. The Christ-life has to be re-lived to be understood. Perhaps it is only then that the part of sacrifice is fully appreciated in the scheme of things.

Granted then that we who are now in the thirties and forties have made a mistake, what is there to be done about it? There's not much that *we* can do. So it falls to youth to put things right. What their seniors have let drop by being slow, lazy, flabby, compromising, and not sufficiently adventurous, the men and women of this generation have got to pick up by being full of faith and very much on the spot indeed. Not only have they to be tingling with Christian idealism themselves, but they must be prepared to radiate this burning heat to others. Nothing but a flaming love for Christ and for those for whom Christ died can do this. If Christian youth were to energize for its spiritual purpose with the vigour which pagan youth puts into its material endeavour, we should have no reason to fear an even temporary eclipse. It is a pity that we can't be persuaded to do for truth what our enemies are prepared to do for error. It is a pity, but not an irremediable pity: we can begin again, we can pick out those things that our adversaries are particularly good at, we can give to these natural virtues a Christian twist, and outdo the opposition at their own game. After all the natural virtues are ours. We can show to the world that Christianity is still a Youth Movement, and that the great thing about a movement is that it moves. We have sat still too long, and the tide has gone out. But the great thing about a tide is that it can come in again.

WHY NOT TRY THE GOSPEL?

FROM ALMOST any book or play that has been written within the last twenty years by any except positively religious writers you could choose a dozen quotations to illustrate the prevailing disillusion and lack of hope. Mr. Noel Coward who always puts his finger on the mood of the moment makes his weary decadents sing: "Chaos and confusion. . . . People seem to lose their way. . . . What is there to strive for, love or keep alive for?" And we answer "What indeed—for those who face the wrong way?"

The world has lost its bearings. By the skin of its teeth it has been saved from toppling over one of the worst precipices that have ever threatened its safety. And now it is heading straight towards another. It is time that the world went back and looked up a better route. When a man is not sure of his road, he can either go on and trust to luck or else retrace his steps till he comes to a signpost or a guide. The modern world has decided to trust to luck. It does not want to begin again. All right. But don't let it say that there were no signposts or guides. There are.

If the world would risk being bored by the subject, it could hardly do better than investigate the purpose of man. In the rush of supplying his needs, this matter has been overlooked. The nearer we approximate to the idea as originally conceived, the more fully is our chief need—the need for happiness—realized. So long as a civilization is under the delusion that its members are created for success or pleasure, or even for such noble ends as intellectual good, family life, peace among men—ideals certainly to be aimed at—it is doomed to disappointment. In the ordering of mankind there is more than mind and body to provide for, and unless progress means progress towards God it can never mean more than prosperity, which is a very doubtful good indeed. So during periods when the destinies of nations lie in the hands of men whose vision is limited to what is temporal, the universe has every reason to feel alarmed. Economic and social ideals cannot carry a continent far when the ultimate ideal is ignored. There can be but one security, and we have come to the stage now when the grounds of this security are denied. The outlook is not rosy.

Like travellers who have missed their way let us get back to the beginning and examine the map. Our map-reading powers have been prejudiced since first we took the wrong turning in the garden, but this is no excuse because in the shape of the Gospel a signpost has appeared out of the mist. Or rather it is the Gospel in the shape of a signpost, because in this particular instance it happens to look like one. There is nothing that so resembles a signpost as a gibbet. There is no way so unmistakable as the way that is pointed by the arms of the Cross. But that is just the way that the world refuses to go.

Forgetting the world for a moment we can take that member of it with whom we are most intimate. I call myself a Christian. My standards, principles, ideals—all my approaches in fact—take not only their colour but their meaning and inspiration from the Gospel. At least that is the theory. Right. I am familiar with the Cross. I know what it stands for. I live in the shadow of it. Even—I ought to be able to say this—even, I am most myself when hanging from the Cross . . . as Christ whose name I bear as Christian was most Himself when hanging from the Cross. In the last analysis the Cross is the test. It is what a signpost is there for: it marks the parting of the ways: it is literally the crux of my life. All this sounds very fine, but probably very few of us believe it; we write it off as a preacher's flourish. The words of the Gospel are not a preacher's flourish. Listen to this: "He that is not with me is against me . . . he that taketh not up his cross is not worthy of me." Whatever the guilt of the world in by-passing the Cross, there is no mistaking my own responsibility. I am a Christian. I ought to know my obligations down to the last full-stop. I do, and this makes it worse: I have not so much ignored it as wrapped it up in cotton wool and carried it on padded shoulders. I, within the Church, have made a greater mistake than those outside it: where the purblind leaders of the world have relied upon social ethics without Christianity, I have experimented in Christian ethics without the Cross.

To conclude: the whole Christian must be surrendered to the whole Christ. The Christian may not select what of the Gospel he wishes to follow and what he prefers to leave alone. "I believe in forgiving people, but of course chastity makes no appeal to me whatever." Nor may the Christian say what of himself he wishes to give to God and what he wants to deny Him. "I am ready enough to provide for the support of my pastors, but I am not going to be dictated to as to the justice of the steps I take to do so." It is not only the religious who belongs to God. A man is not bound to give up his possessions, but he is at least expected to acknowledge that they are God's before they are his. For a man to be a Christian in anything but name, the whole of life—as he enjoys it or suffers it or merely drifts through it—must come under the cover of religion. His working life, his social life, his family life, his intellectual, sporting, artistic, sleeping and waking life . . . the whole thing is referred with greater or lesser conscious direction (according to the degree of holiness in the subject) back again to God. What

is there of me that I hide from God? What pleasure?
What person? What desire? Only if I can run right through
the catalogue and say that God is Lord of *all* am I in any
real sense a follower of Christ.

"And I, if I be lifted up, will draw all things unto myself."
Draw all that I am and have, Lord. Draw all nations also
to Thyself.

ERECTI MORIAMUR

THIS, THE last section of the book, is meant to be a sort of signature tune. Or, more properly, the kind of thing that is played while the audience is leaving the show: a collection of tunes strung together and reminding the people of what they have just heard. If the foregoing pages have any message at all it is an invitation to face facts and not to lie down under modern pressures or ancient prejudices. There is such a lot that we take for granted and never for a moment question. We have accepted from infancy a whole crop of ideas which we have never shaken up for ourselves or held to the light of our particular vision: we have never examined them in the mind of Christ. Now that *We Die Standing Up* is finished I very much want to write a companion volume called *We Live With Our Eyes Open*. The doctrine of let's-be-tough is not the whole burden of this book, but it is a good part of it. The doctrine of look-for-the-light is a more important part, and whether it reveals itself in what has to do with human intercourse or with the relationship between the soul and God, it is the side of life which we have most need to get right. Watching and praying gets us further than the use of sackcloth and ashes, because it is through prayer that we shall see the value of penance. Indeed it is through prayer that we shall not only see the pitfalls of toughness but we shall see also the pinnacles of God's creation. We shall see everything from on top: we shall get, through prayer, the saint's-eye view. We have sometimes to climb a tower in order to see life spread out before us as it really is. Its beauties, on the flat, get crowded out.

163

Six years of war have accustomed people to the idea of physical endurance. Softness is, for the moment, out of fashion. We are a little proud of being able to do things for ourselves. "I came all the way by bicycle. Twelve miles? That's nothing." But the trouble is that with the effort to brace one's muscles to meet the needs of the day, there has come about a corresponding stiffening of the mind. Power politics have invaded the region of the soul. Altered social conditions have interfered with intellectual standards and have gone a good way towards upsetting moral and spiritual values. Out of all this have come power ideologies. What place has the word LOVE in the programme of, say, world peace? Or, more immediately, in the programme of domestic peace? Drop the word LOVE into the columns of any newspaper and see what effect it has on its context. It is a dynamic word at all times, and you will find that it will make as much noise as it has ever done, but its note will be the note of the saxophone and not the harp. In its Hollywood sense it may have a meaning for the world at large, but certainly not in any other.

We have then to be tough in our determination to put the first things first, and to meet the world's philosophies with a toughness at least as obstinate as theirs. We have to be no less tough in dealing with ourselves. Not physically merely, but much more morally. No excuses, no compromises, no trailing away into the land of easy options and deadening slogans. We must keep our eyes open all the time, and *look*. Christ means the Cross, and there are no mists on Calvary. If you watch and pray you won't have the face to say you've never really seen the issues in their true terms. You won't have the face to plead the easy way out. *Erecti moriamur*. We have got to die, so let us die standing up.

If it were simply a matter of dying perhaps we could step

up and meet it with a certain practised *expertise*. There is
no glamour like the fighting finish. But in actual fact it is
the drawn out business of life that we have to face, and for
most of us this is far worse. It means fighting every inch
of life's boredoms and petty pinprick worries, it means
fighting ourselves and our moods and our manias and our
phobias and our fixations. There is no glamour about
this, no applause, no appreciable victories. Die standing
up? Certainly, but we live standing up as well: we sleep
with our boots on.

I once asked Father Bede Jarrett what was his favourite
virtue, and he said: "After charity, I suppose fortitude . . .
but, mind you, the day-to-day kind, and none of your shot-
gun stuff." He himself of course had both. We may pretend to look down upon the shot-gun stuff but it is after
all the effect, though the spectacular effect, of the spun out
courage that has gone before. It was no surprise, therefore,
to those who knew the manner of his life to learn the manner
of his death. Father Bede went on until, literally, he dropped.
I call that dying with your boots on. Though he himself
may have had little use for the showy nature of his finish,
there is no reason why we should think the same. Happy
is the man who so lives that death may find him spiritually,
and even physically, on his feet.

CPSIA information can be obtained
at www.ICGtesting.com
Printed in the USA
BVHW090907281220
596438BV00010B/647